CPC Exam Study Guide

The Step-by-Step Approach to Mastering the Exam and Launching Your Career in Medical Coding | 300 Questions and Answers Included

Anthony Alfred

Table of content

Chapter 1: Introduction to CPC Exam and Medical Coding

- Overview of Certified Professional Coder (CPC) exam

Medical coders' knowledge and abilities are rigorously and thoroughly evaluated on the Certified Professional Coder (CPC) exam. The American Academy of Professional Coders (AAPC) administers the test, which measures candidates' ability to accurately record diagnoses, treatments, and services rendered in healthcare settings.

It takes five hours and forty minutes to finish the 150 multiple-choice questions on the CPC exam. The exam covers a wide range of subjects, including, among others, anatomy and physiology, coding standards, CPT, ICD-10-CM, and coding for procedures. The questions are made to assess the candidate's understanding of the coding policies, processes, and norms as well as their capacity to decipher intricate medical records and select the appropriate codes.

Candidates must have completed an AAPC-approved coding program or have at least two years of coding experience in a medical context in order to sit for the CPC exam. They must also follow the AAPC's code of conduct and obtain continuing education credits to keep their credentials current.

The CPC exam is a difficult test that necessitates much planning and study. Many candidates decide to sign up for a CPC exam preparation course, which gives them a thorough overview of the exam's subject matter, format, and rules.

To assist students in getting ready for the exam, these courses frequently contain study materials, practice exams, and internet resources.

For medical coders, passing the CPC exam is a noteworthy achievement that may lead to new jobs. Candidates who succeed are awarded the CPC credential, which attests to their knowledge and skill in medical coding. CPCs can operate in a variety of settings, including hospitals, clinics, doctor's offices, and insurance firms. They are highly sought after in the healthcare sector.

To sum up, the Certified Professional Coder (CPC) exam is an exacting and thorough evaluation of a medical coder's expertise in medical coding. The exam covers a wide range of subjects, including, among others, anatomy and physiology, coding standards, CPT, ICD-10-CM, and coding for procedures. For medical coders, passing the CPC exam is a noteworthy achievement that may lead to new jobs. Candidates who succeed are awarded the CPC credential, which attests to their knowledge and skill in medical coding.

- Importance of medical coding in healthcare industry

Medical coding is an essential component of the healthcare industry. It is the process of translating medical procedures, diagnoses, and services into standardized codes that are used for billing, reimbursement, and data collection. Medical coders play a critical role in the healthcare industry by ensuring the accuracy and completeness of medical records, facilitating the billing process, and providing valuable data for research and analysis.

Accurate medical coding is crucial for healthcare providers and insurers to receive proper reimbursement for services rendered. Medical coders use various coding systems, such as ICD-10-CM, CPT, and HCPCS Level II, to assign the appropriate codes for procedures and services performed. These codes are then used to determine the amount of reimbursement that healthcare providers receive from insurance companies and government payers.

In addition to facilitating the billing process, medical coding is also essential for maintaining accurate patient records. Medical coders ensure that medical records are complete and accurate by reviewing documentation from healthcare providers and assigning the appropriate codes. This information is critical for healthcare providers to make informed decisions about patient care and treatment options.

Medical coding also provides valuable data for research and analysis. Healthcare organizations and government agencies use medical coding data to track disease trends, evaluate healthcare quality, and identify areas for improvement. Medical coding data is also used to monitor healthcare costs, develop new medical treatments, and improve patient outcomes.

The importance of medical coding has become increasingly evident in recent years, as healthcare costs continue to rise, and healthcare policies and regulations become more complex. Medical coding is essential for healthcare providers to receive proper reimbursement for services rendered, maintain accurate patient records, and provide valuable data for research and analysis. The demand for skilled medical coders has also increased in recent years, as healthcare organizations seek to improve the accuracy and efficiency of their coding processes. Certified Professional Coders (CPCs) are highly sought after in the healthcare industry, as they demonstrate their expertise and proficiency in medical coding. CPCs are trained to ensure the accuracy and completeness of medical records, facilitate the billing process, and provide valuable data for research and analysis.

In conclusion, medical coding plays a critical role in the healthcare industry, ensuring the accuracy and completeness of medical records, facilitating the billing process, and providing valuable data for research and analysis. Accurate medical coding is essential for healthcare providers and insurers to receive proper reimbursement for services rendered. The demand for skilled medical coders has increased in recent years, as healthcare organizations seek to improve the accuracy and efficiency of their coding processes. Certified Professional Coders (CPCs) are highly sought after in the healthcare industry, as they demonstrate their expertise and proficiency in medical coding.

Chapter 2: Medical Terminology and Anatomy

- Fundamentals of medical terminology

The lingo used in medicine is called medical terminology. It is a specific language that medical experts use to talk about the human body, illnesses, and remedies.A solid understanding of medical terminology is essential for medical coders to accurately assign codes for diagnoses and procedures.

Medical terminology is based on Latin and Greek roots, prefixes, and suffixes. Understanding these building blocks of medical terminology is crucial for deciphering complex medical terms. For example, the prefix "hypo-" means "under," while the suffix "-itis" means "inflammation." Therefore, the term "hypothyroiditis" means "inflammation of the thyroid gland due to an underactive thyroid."

Medical terminology is also divided into body systems, such as the cardiovascular, respiratory, and digestive systems. Each body system has its own set of terms and abbreviations that medical coders must be familiar with. For example, terms related to the cardiovascular system include "atrium," "ventricle," "artery," and "vein."

In addition to understanding the building blocks and body systems of medical terminology, medical coders must also be familiar with medical abbreviations and acronyms. Medical abbreviations are used to save time and space in medical documentation, but they can be confusing and potentially dangerous if not properly understood. Medical coders must be able to decipher medical abbreviations and ensure that they are accurately translated into codes.

One of the most effective ways to learn medical terminology is through memorization and repetition. Medical coders must be familiar with a large number of terms and abbreviations, so it is essential to practice regularly to build a strong foundation of medical terminology knowledge.

In conclusion, medical terminology is the language of medicine and is essential for medical coders to accurately assign codes for diagnoses and procedures. Understanding the building blocks of medical terminology, body systems, and medical abbreviations is crucial for deciphering complex medical terms. Medical coders must practice regularly to build a strong foundation of medical terminology knowledge and be able to accurately translate medical terms and abbreviations into codes.

- Common medical abbreviations

Common medical abbreviations are an important part of medical terminology and play a critical role in communication between healthcare providers. Medical abbreviations are used to save time and space in medical documentation, but it is important to use them correctly and in compliance with industry standards.

One common type of medical abbreviation is the acronym, which is a word formed from the first letter of each word in a phrase. For example, "MRI" stands for "magnetic resonance imaging," and "CPR" stands for "cardiopulmonary resuscitation." Acronyms are often used to refer to medical procedures, tests, or conditions.

Another type of medical abbreviation is the initialism, which is similar to an acronym but is pronounced by saying each letter separately. For example, "COPD" stands for "chronic obstructive pulmonary disease," and "TB" stands for "tuberculosis." Initialisms are often used to refer to medical conditions or diseases.

Medical abbreviations can also include symbols, such as the "+" sign, which is used to indicate a positive result on a test or screening. Other symbols, such as the "#" sign, may be used to indicate a number or quantity.

It is important to note that medical abbreviations can sometimes be confusing or ambiguous, and can lead to errors in communication if used incorrectly. For this reason, it is important to use approved abbreviations and to clarify any abbreviations that may be unclear or unfamiliar to others.

To ensure accuracy and compliance with industry standards, healthcare providers should reference approved lists of medical abbreviations and avoid using non-standard abbreviations. The lingo used in medicine is called medical terminology. It is a specific language that medical experts use to talk about the human body, illnesses, and remedies.

In addition to using approved abbreviations, healthcare providers should also take care to avoid using abbreviations that may be easily misinterpreted or confused with other abbreviations. For example, "IU" can be used to indicate "international units" or "intravenous use," so it is important to provide context to avoid confusion.

Overall, common medical abbreviations play an important role in medical documentation and communication between healthcare providers. However, it is important to use them correctly and in compliance with industry standards to ensure accuracy and avoid errors in communication. By using approved abbreviations and providing context when necessary, healthcare providers can ensure clear and effective communication with their colleagues and patients.

- Anatomy and physiology basics

Medical coding is built on the principles of anatomy and physiology. Medical coders must have a fundamental understanding of human anatomy and physiology in order to correctly assign codes for diagnosis and treatments.
The study of the composition and arrangement of the human body is known as anatomy. It covers the examination of the body's systems, tissues, and organs. Medical coders must have a rudimentary understanding of human anatomy in order to correctly assign diagnoses and procedures to codes. For instance, understanding the various medical diseases and processes relating to the various types of bodily tissues, such as epithelial, connective, muscular, and nerve tissue, is crucial.
The study of physiology examines how the body works. In order to sustain health and homeostasis, the cells, tissues, organs, and systems of the body are studied, as well as how they interact with one another. Medical coders must be familiar with the fundamental physiology of the human body in order to correctly assign codes for diagnosis and procedures. For instance, it's crucial to grasp the cardiovascular system's operation in order to comprehend heart and blood vessel-related diseases as well as the techniques employed to identify and treat them.
Medical words relating to anatomy and physiology are also essential knowledge for medical coders. Latin and Greek roots, prefixes, and suffixes are frequently used in medical terminology pertaining to anatomy and physiology. It's crucial to

comprehend the meaning of these roots, prefixes, and suffixes in order to decode complicated medical terminology. A sickness of the heart muscle is referred to as "cardiomyopathy," for instance, where "cardio" stands for the "heart," "myo" for the "muscle," and "pathy" for the "disease."

Anatomy and physiology are also important for understanding medical test results and reports. Medical coders must be able to read and interpret medical reports and understand the terminology used in these reports. For example, a medical report may include results from a diagnostic test, such as an electrocardiogram (ECG), which measures the electrical activity of the heart. Understanding the anatomy and physiology of the heart is crucial for interpreting the results of an ECG and accurately assigning codes for diagnoses and procedures related to the heart.

In conclusion, a basic understanding of human anatomy and physiology is essential for medical coders to accurately assign codes for diagnoses and procedures. Medical coders must be familiar with the different types of body tissues, organs, and systems, as well as the basic physiology of the human body. They must also be familiar with medical terminology related to anatomy and physiology and be able to interpret medical reports and test results accurately.

Chapter 3: ICD-10-CM Coding

- Introduction to ICD-10-CM coding system

Medical diagnoses and diseases are coded using the International Classification of Diseases, 10th Revision, Clinical Modification (ICD-10-CM). In the US, healthcare providers, insurers, and governmental organizations utilize it to record and analyze healthcare data, guarantee proper billing, and get payment for medical services.

The ICD-10-CM coding system is divided into chapters based on various bodily systems, including the digestive, circulatory, and respiratory systems. Each chapter has codes that list the diseases and diagnoses associated with that body system. The alphanumeric codes can contain up to seven characters.

An ICD-10-CM code's first three characters identify the ailment or diagnosis's category, while the fourth, fifth, and sixth characters offer more specific information. The episode of care or the condition's state, such as whether it is the first or subsequent contact, are indicated by the seventh character.

The specificity of the ICD-10-CM coding system is one of its main advantages. The system has many codes that make it possible to document medical diagnoses and symptoms in greater accuracy and detail. This can aid insurance companies in fairly calculating payments for medical services, as well as healthcare professionals in understanding and treating their patients.

However, the ICD-10-CM coding system's improved specificity can also make it trickier and more difficult to use. Healthcare professionals must receive training on how to utilize the system correctly and must keep up with any adjustments to the codes and recommendations.

Other coding systems, such as the Current Procedural Terminology (CPT) coding system and the Healthcare Common Procedure Coding System (HCPCS) Level II coding system, are used in medical documentation and billing in addition to the ICD-10-CM coding system. Each coding system has a distinct function and needs specialized knowledge and training to be utilized correctly. The ICD-10-CM coding system, which is used to record and examine medical diagnoses and disorders, is generally regarded as an essential part of the healthcare sector. Although its specialization enables more precise and thorough recording, using it successfully also necessitates specialized training and knowledge. Healthcare providers can assure correct billing and compensation for medical services as well as improve patient care by adhering to the rules and regulations established by the system.

- ICD-10-CM coding guidelines

Medical coders utilize the ICD-10-CM coding guidelines as a collection of rules and conventions to assign precise and comprehensive codes for diagnosis and medical conditions. The Centers for Medicare and Medicaid Services (CMS) publish the standards, which are frequently revised to reflect changes in medical language and coding conventions.

The correct use of codes, code sequencing, and coding for multiple illnesses are only a few of the many subjects covered by the ICD-10-CM coding rules. To guarantee that medical records are accurate, comprehensive, and comply with healthcare legislation, medical coders must adhere to these rules.

The proper usage of codes is one of the most crucial ICD-10-CM coding requirements. The most specific code that fully captures the patient's medical condition must be chosen by medical coders. In order to correctly determine the appropriate code for each condition, coders must be knowledgeable about the various coding system levels of detail.

The order in which the codes are used is another crucial component of ICD-10-CM coding guidelines. For proper billing and reimbursement, it's crucial that the codes are allocated in the right order. To guarantee that the primary diagnosis is recorded first and that any secondary diagnoses are listed in the proper order, medical coders must adhere to strict sequencing criteria.

Multiple conditions are coded according to ICD-10-CM coding standards. Medical coders must be able to correctly assign codes to patients who suffer from a variety of ailments, whether or not they are connected in any way. Coders must adhere to certain rules in these situations to guarantee that all pertinent criteria are correctly coded.

Additionally, specific instructions on how to code for various medical illnesses and treatments are provided in the ICD-10-CM coding rules. For instance, the recommendations offer particular codes and coding criteria for ailments like diabetes, hypertension, and heart disease. Additionally, they offer advice on how to code operations like surgery, radiography, and lab tests.

In order to guarantee that medical records are accurate and comprehensive, medical coders must be conversant with and strictly adhere to the ICD-10-CM coding criteria. Inaccurate billing and reimbursement may come from not adhering to these rules, and there may also be potential legal and regulatory repercussions.

In conclusion, medical coders use the ICD-10-CM coding guidelines as a set of rules and conventions to assign precise and comprehensive codes for diagnoses and medical conditions. The instructions include a wide range of subjects, such as how to use codes correctly, how to order codes, and how to code for various situations. To guarantee that medical records are accurate, comprehensive, and consistent with healthcare regulations, medical coders must rigorously adhere to these rules.

- Coding conventions and guidelines for specific chapters

A crucial component of medical coding is the use of coding rules and recommendations for particular chapters. According to the body system or disease being classified, the International Classification of Diseases, 10th Revision, Clinical Modification (ICD-10-CM) is broken down into chapters. Medical coders must adhere to specific standards and criteria for each chapter in order to correctly assign codes for diagnoses and medical problems. Coding conventions and rules that are relevant to each chapter include detailed instructions on how to utilize codes correctly, sequence codes, and code for numerous circumstances within each chapter. For instance, the ICD-10-CM's Chapter 1 has codes for specific viral and parasitic disorders. Detailed instructions on how to code for infectious diseases, including the use of additional codes to identify the causative organism and the kind of infection, are provided in the coding rules for Chapter 1.

The ICD-10-CM's Chapter 2 also has codes for neoplasms and tumors. The coding recommendations for Chapter 2 include detailed guidance on how to sequence codes for neoplasms that have metastasized to other sections of the body as well as how to code for primary and secondary tumors.

The ICD-10-CM's Chapter 3 contains codes for conditions affecting the blood and organs that produce blood. Anemia, hemophilia, and other blood disorders are specifically described in the coding guidelines for Chapter 3 with detailed instructions. Additionally, these standards give detailed advice on how to code for blood transfusions and other procedures using blood.

Endocrine, nutritional, and metabolic illnesses are coded in Chapter 4 of the ICD-10-CM. The coding standards for Chapter 4 give detailed guidance on how to code for endocrine illnesses like diabetes, thyroid issues, and others. Additionally, these standards give detailed advice on how to code for nutritional diseases such as malnutrition.

Mental, behavioral, and neurodevelopmental disorders are coded in ICD-10-CM Chapter 5. How to code for disorders like anxiety, depression, and other mental health issues is made clear in the Chapter 5 coding rules. Additionally, these recommendations offer detailed guidance on how to code for neurodevelopmental conditions like autism and attention deficit hyperactivity disorder (ADHD).

Chapter-specific coding conventions and recommendations offer guidance on the proper use of modifiers, combination codes, and other coding standards in addition to offering explicit instructions on how to code for various conditions. To correctly assign codes for diagnosis and medical problems, medical coders need to be conversant with certain norms and rules.

Finally, it should be noted that chapter-specific coding rules and guidelines are a crucial component of medical coding. These recommendations include detailed advice on how to utilize codes correctly, arrange them in the right order, and code for various illnesses within each chapter of the ICD-10-CM. These rules must be understood by medical coders in order to assign diagnoses and medical conditions the proper codes.

Chapter 4: CPT Coding

- Introduction to Current Procedural Terminology (CPT) coding system

A standardized approach for describing medical procedures and services offered by healthcare professionals is called Current Procedural Terminology (CPT). The American Medical Association (AMA) oversees the system, which is used in the US for billing and reimbursement needs.

According to the kind of service offered, CPT codes are divided into sections such evaluation and management, anesthesia, surgery, and radiography. Each CPT code comprises a description of the treatment or service rendered, as well as any additional details like the procedure's length and complexity.

Healthcare providers use CPT codes to record and bill for the services they offer, and insurance companies use them to decide how much to pay for those services. Every year, the codes are changed to reflect advancements in medical techniques and practices.

The use of modifiers is a crucial aspect of the CPT coding system. Modifiers are extra codes that can be used to add details about an operation or service. A modifier might be used, for instance, to say that a procedure was carried out at numerous locations or that a patient received a service in a telehealth environment. To ensure appropriate invoicing and reimbursement, it's crucial to apply modifiers effectively and in accordance with established industry standards.

The usage of unbundling codes is a crucial factor in CPT coding. Using numerous codes to describe a method or service that should be covered by a single, comprehensive code is known as "unbundling codes." This could lead to overbilling and is against industry norms.

Healthcare practitioners should refer to approved CPT code lists and refrain from utilizing non-standard codes or modifiers to maintain accuracy and industry compliance. For healthcare professionals to use the CPT coding system appropriately and efficiently, the AMA offers materials and training.

Other coding systems, such as the Healthcare Common Procedure Coding System (HCPCS) Level II coding system and the International Classification of Diseases, 10th Revision, Clinical Modification (ICD-10-CM) coding system, are used in medical documentation and billing in addition to the CPT coding system. Each coding system has a distinct function and needs specialized knowledge and training to be utilized correctly.

Overall, the CPT coding system, which is used to record and charge for medical operations and services, is an essential part of the healthcare sector. Although its controlled and standardized approach enables precise invoicing and reimbursement, using it successfully also necessitates specialized knowledge and training. Healthcare providers can assure correct billing and compensation for medical services as well as improve patient care by adhering to the rules and regulations established by the system.

- CPT coding guidelines

CPT coding guidelines are a set of rules and conventions used by medical coders to accurately assign codes for medical procedures and services. The Current Procedural Terminology (CPT) code set is published by the American Medical Association (AMA) and is used by healthcare providers and medical coders to report medical procedures and services to insurance providers and government agencies.

CPT coding guidelines cover a wide range of topics, including the correct use of codes, coding for multiple procedures, and coding for modifiers. Medical coders must follow these guidelines to ensure that medical records are accurate, complete, and compliant with healthcare regulations.

One of the most important aspects of CPT coding guidelines is the correct use of codes. Medical coders must select the most specific code that accurately describes the medical procedure or service that was performed. This means that coders must be familiar with the different levels of specificity in the coding system and be able to accurately identify the correct code for each procedure or service.

CPT coding guidelines also cover coding for multiple procedures. Medical coders must be able to accurately assign codes for patients who have had multiple medical procedures performed during a single visit. In these cases, coders must follow specific guidelines to ensure that all relevant procedures are accurately coded.

Another important aspect of CPT coding guidelines is coding for modifiers. Modifiers are two-digit codes that are added to CPT codes to provide additional information about the procedure or service that was performed. For example, a modifier may indicate that a procedure was performed on both the left and right sides of the body. Medical coders must be familiar with the different types of modifiers and know how to use them correctly to accurately report medical procedures and services.

CPT coding guidelines also provide specific guidance on coding for certain medical procedures and services. For example, the guidelines provide specific codes and coding rules for procedures such as surgery, radiology, and laboratory tests. They also provide guidance on coding for services such as physical therapy, occupational therapy, and speech therapy.

Medical coders must be familiar with the CPT coding guidelines and follow them closely to ensure that medical records are accurate, complete, and compliant with healthcare regulations. Failure to follow these guidelines can result in inaccurate billing and reimbursement, as well as potential legal and regulatory issues.

In conclusion, CPT coding guidelines are a set of rules and conventions used by medical coders to accurately assign codes for medical procedures and services. The guidelines cover a wide range of topics, including the correct use of codes, coding for multiple procedures, and coding for modifiers. Medical coders must follow these guidelines closely to ensure that medical records are accurate, complete, and compliant with healthcare regulations.

- Coding procedures for different specialties

Coding procedures for different specialties is a critical component of medical documentation and billing. Different medical specialties require different codes and guidelines to accurately document and bill for the procedures and services provided.

For example, in the field of cardiology, there are specific codes used to document and bill for procedures such as echocardiograms, cardiac catheterizations, and pacemaker implantation.

In the field of orthopedics, there are specific codes used to document and bill for procedures such as joint replacements, fracture care, and arthroscopic surgery.

These codes may also require the use of modifiers to provide additional information about the procedure or service provided.

In the field of gastroenterology, there are specific codes used to document and bill for procedures such as colonoscopies, upper endoscopies, and biopsy procedures. These codes may also require the use of modifiers to indicate additional information about the procedure, such as whether it was performed on multiple sites.

Other medical specialties, such as neurology, dermatology, and ophthalmology, also have specific codes and guidelines for documenting and billing for procedures and services. It is important for healthcare providers to stay up-to-date with changes and updates to these codes and guidelines to ensure accurate billing and reimbursement.

In addition to specialty-specific codes and guidelines, healthcare providers may also use general codes and guidelines for procedures and services that are not specific to a particular specialty. For example, the CPT coding system includes codes for evaluation and management services, laboratory procedures, and radiology procedures, which can be used across a variety of medical specialties.

To ensure accuracy and compliance with industry standards, healthcare providers should reference approved lists of codes and guidelines for their particular specialty, and should avoid using non-standard codes or modifiers. They should also provide clear and detailed documentation of the procedures and services provided to ensure accurate billing and reimbursement.

Overall, coding procedures for different specialties is an important aspect of medical documentation and billing. By following the guidelines and standards set forth by the coding systems and industry organizations, healthcare providers can ensure accurate billing and reimbursement for their services, and can provide better care to their patients.

Chapter 5: HCPCS Level II Coding

- An introduction to Level II coding for the Healthcare Common Procedure Coding System (HCPCS)

Medical procedures and services not covered by the Current Procedural Terminology (CPT) code set are reported using the Healthcare Common Procedure Coding System (HCPCS) Level II coding. The Centers for Medicare and Medicaid Services (CMS) publishes the HCPCS Level II code set, which is largely used for reporting medical operations and services to governmental organizations and insurance companies.

Durable medical equipment, prosthetics, orthotics, and supplies (DMEPOS) and other medical services are the two major divisions of the HCPCS Level II coding system. Medical equipment like wheelchairs and walkers as well as medical supplies like bandages and catheters are coded under the DMEPOS category. Codes covering medical procedures and services that are not covered by the CPT code set, such as ambulance services, chemotherapy, and radiation therapy, are included in the category of other medical services.

The HCPCS Level II coding system's usage of alpha-numeric codes is one of its main characteristics. Four or five numbers are followed by a single letter in HCPCS Level II codes. The numbers offer further details about the particular procedure or service being recorded, while the letter designates the code's primary category.

Modifier use is a crucial component of HCPCS Level II code. HCPCS Level II codes can have two-digit modifiers appended to them to give more details about the process or service being recorded. For instance, a modifier can say that the patient received a specific piece of equipment on a leasing basis rather than an outright purchase.

The HCPCS Level II coding system must be understood by medical coders, and they must be proficient at accurately assigning codes for medical operations and services. This necessitates a detailed comprehension of the many code categories, as well as the particular codes and modifiers utilized in each category.

The main purpose of the HCPCS Level II coding system is to report medical operations and services to regulatory bodies and insurance companies. In order to make sure that medical records are accurate, comprehensive, and consistent with healthcare rules, medical coders must be knowledgeable with the particular coding criteria of each agency or provider.

Medical coders may also use other coding systems, such as the International Classification of Diseases, 10th Revision, Clinical Modification (ICD-10-CM) code set, in addition to the HCPCS Level II coding system. To guarantee that medical records are correctly tagged and reported, medical coders are required to be knowledgeable with all coding systems used in their line of work.

In conclusion, the Current Procedural Terminology (CPT) code set does not cover all medical operations and services, hence a set of codes called Healthcare Common Procedure Coding System (HCPCS) Level II coding is used to report those. Durable medical equipment, prosthetics, orthotics, and supplies (DMEPOS) and other medical services are the two major divisions of the HCPCS Level II coding system. A single letter is followed by four or five numbers in an HCPCS Level II code, and additional codes may be added to the code to provide more details about the treatment or service being reported. To guarantee that medical records are accurate, comprehensive, and consistent with healthcare rules, medical coders must be knowledgeable with the HCPCS Level II coding system and have the ability to appropriately assign codes for medical operations and services.

- HCPCS Level II coding guidelines

In the United States, the Healthcare Common Procedure Coding System (HCPCS) Level II coding system is used to document and bill for medical supplies, equipment, and services not covered by the Current Procedural Terminology (CPT) coding system. The Centers for Medicare and Medicaid Services (CMS) maintains HCPCS Level II codes, which are used for billing and reimbursement by healthcare providers, insurance companies, and government agencies.

HCPCS Level II codes are classified by the type of supply or equipment, such as durable medical equipment, prosthetics, orthotics, and supplies. Each code contains a description of the item or service offered, as well as extra information such as quantity and length of use.

The usage of modifiers is an important part of HCPCS Level II coding. Modifiers are extra codes that can be used to convey more information about a supply or equipment item, such as its size or color. Modifiers can also be used to indicate whether a supply or piece of equipment is new or used, rented or purchased.

The use of National Drug Codes (NDCs) for drugs and vaccines is another significant factor in HCPCS Level II coding. NDCs are unique codes provided by the Food and Drug Administration (FDA) to each drug or vaccination and are used for invoicing and reimbursement.

Healthcare practitioners should use approved lists of HCPCS Level II codes and avoid using non-standard codes or modifiers to ensure accuracy and compliance with industry standards. The CMS provides materials and training to healthcare practitioners to ensure they are correctly and successfully using the HCPCS Level II coding system.

Other coding systems used in medical documentation and billing, in addition to the HCPCS Level II coding system, include the CPT coding system and the International Classification of Diseases, 10th Revision, Clinical Modification (ICD-10-CM) code system. Each coding system serves a distinct purpose and necessitates specialized knowledge and training to be used properly.

Overall, the HCPCS Level II coding system is an important part of the healthcare business since it is used to document and bill for medical supplies, equipment, and services that are not covered by the CPT code system. Its structured and standardized approach enables precise invoicing and compensation, but it also demands specific expertise and training to operate efficiently. By adhering to the system's principles and regulations, healthcare professionals can ensure correct invoicing and reimbursement for medical services, as well as deliver better care to their patients.

- Coding procedures for supplies, equipment, and other non-physician services

Medical coding procedures for supplies, equipment, and other non-physician services are critical. The Healthcare Common Procedure Coding System (HCPCS) Level II coding system is often used to report medical procedures and services that are not covered by the Current Procedural Terminology (CPT) code set.

HCPCS Level II codes are used to report supplies and equipment in the category of durable medical equipment, prosthetics, orthotics, and supplies (DMEPOS). This category includes codes for medical equipment like wheelchairs and walkers, as well as medical supplies like bandages and catheters. Medical coders must be knowledgeable with the specific codes used in this category and know how to assign codes appropriately for the items and equipment delivered to the patient.

Non-physician services, such as ambulance services and physical therapy, are reported under the other medical services category using HCPCS Level II codes. This category contains codes for a wide variety of medical treatments and services not covered by the CPT code set. Medical coders must be knowledgeable with the specific codes used in this category and understand how to assign codes appropriately for the treatments and services offered to the patient.

Ensure that the correct codes are issued is one of the most difficult difficulties in coding systems for supplies, equipment, and other non-physician services.

Medical coders must be familiar with the many types of codes and be able to determine the precise code that corresponds to the treatment or service delivered. Furthermore, medical coders must be knowledgeable with the rules and regulations that govern the use of these codes, as well as any special requirements of the insurance provider or government agency to which the codes are reported.

Modifiers are another key part of coding methods for supplies, equipment, and other non-physician services. Modifiers are two-digit codes appended to HCPCS Level II codes to provide more information about the process or service being reported. A modifier, for example, may indicate that a specific piece of equipment was rented to the patient rather than purchased entirely. To effectively report medical procedures and services, medical coders must be aware with the many types of modifiers and how to utilize them correctly. Medical coders must also be conversant with the documentation standards for supplies, equipment, and other non-physician services. This includes ensuring that all required documentation, such as invoices and medical records, is correct, full, and in accordance with healthcare rules. Inadequate documentation might lead to erroneous coding and possibly legal and regulatory difficulties. Finally, coding processes for supplies, equipment, and other non-physician services are critical components of medical coding. The HCPCS Level II coding system is often used to report medical procedures and services that are not covered by the CPT code set. Medical coders must understand the precise codes used in DMEPOS and other medical service categories, as well as the rules and regulations that govern their use. They must also be knowledgeable with the various types of modifiers and how to effectively apply them in order to accurately record medical procedures and services. Finally, medical coders must ensure that all relevant paperwork is correct, complete, and in accordance with healthcare rules in order for medical records to be coded and reported accurately.

Chapter 6: Medical Coding Modifiers

- Introduction to coding modifiers

Coding modifiers are extra codes that are used in medical documentation and invoicing to provide more information about a procedure or service. Modifiers are added to codes to indicate that a specific scenario applied to the treatment or service, which may have an impact on reimbursement.

Modifiers can be used to express a wide range of situations. A modifier, for example, may be used to indicate that a procedure was conducted at numerous locations or that a service was offered to a patient via telehealth. Modifiers can also be used to indicate that a procedure was conducted by a different provider or on a different date than was initially scheduled.

Modifiers are significant because they can influence the amount of payment received by a healthcare practitioner for a procedure or service. A modifier, for example, can be used to indicate that a procedure was conducted at various locations, which may result in a higher reimbursement rate.

To ensure appropriate invoicing and reimbursement, it is critical to apply modifiers effectively and in accordance with industry norms. The American Medical Association (AMA) publishes guidelines for the proper use of modifiers, including when each modifier should be used.

In addition to the AMA's rules, healthcare providers should consult approved lists of modifiers for their specific coding system. The Current Procedural Terminology (CPT) coding system, for example, contains a list of modifiers that can be used to convey further information about a process or service.

It is also critical to avoid the practice of code unbundling. The practice of employing numerous codes to describe a method or service that should be contained under a single, comprehensive code is referred to as unbundling codes. This can result in overbilling and is against industry norms.

Coding modifiers are a crucial part of medical documentation and invoicing in general. Healthcare providers may assure accurate billing and compensation for their services and provide better care to their patients by employing modifiers effectively and in accordance with industry norms.

- Common coding modifiers and their uses

Coding modifiers are two-digit codes appended to procedure codes to provide more information about the service being done. These modifiers are used to identify things like the procedure's location, the quantity of services provided, and the sort of provider who provided the service. Understanding basic coding modifiers and their applications is critical for reporting medical operations and services accurately.

Modifier -59 is a typical coding modifier that indicates that a procedure or service was distinct or separate from other services conducted on the same day. This modification is frequently used to report procedures conducted on various anatomical areas or during different sessions.

Modifier -25, which indicates that a separate and unique evaluation and management (E/M) service was delivered on the same day as another operation or service, is another prevalent coding modifier. When a physician offers an E/M service, such as a consultation, on the same day as a procedure or other treatment, this modifier is utilized.

Modifier -50 indicates that a procedure, such as bilateral knee replacements, was performed on both sides of the body. Modifier -51 indicates that numerous operations were conducted within the same session or visit, whereas modifier -52 indicates that a procedure was only partially completed or was discontinued owing to extenuating circumstances.

To offer additional precise information about the procedure being conducted, modifier -59 is frequently used in conjunction with other modifiers. Modifier -59, for example, can be used in conjunction with modifier -51 to indicate that many procedures were done concurrently but were distinct and different from one another.

Modifier -76, which indicates that an operation or service was repeated, is another typical code modifier. This modification is frequently used when an operation or service must be repeated due to a technical mistake or other unforeseen circumstances.

The modifier -80 denotes that a service was performed on an emergency basis. This modifier is used to describe services provided in the event of a medical emergency, such as an emergency appendectomy.

Finally, -91 indicates that a laboratory test was redone on the same day to confirm the accuracy of the initial result. This modifier is frequently employed when the findings of a laboratory test are unexpected or aberrant.

To summarize, recognizing common coding modifiers and their applications is critical for accurately reporting medical procedures and services. Coding modifiers offer additional information about the service being performed, such as the procedure's location, the number of services performed, and the type of provider that provided the service. Modifier -59 is used for unique or separate services, modifier -25 is used for separate E/M services, modifier -50 is used for bilateral operations, and modifier -76 is used for recurrent services. Modifier -51 is used for many procedures, modifier -80 is used for emergency services, and modifier -91 is used for repeated laboratory testing. Medical coders can accurately report medical operations and services and guarantee that medical records are compatible with healthcare standards by understanding these frequent coding modifiers and their uses.

- Rules and guidelines for using coding modifiers

In medical documentation and billing, there are precise regulations and procedures for applying coding modifiers. These regulations and guidelines are in place to ensure correct invoicing and payment, as well as industry compliance.

One key thing to remember when utilizing coding modifiers is to only use them when absolutely necessary. Modifiers should be used to convey more information about a process or service, not to alter reimbursement rates. Only modifiers that are appropriate for the process or service offered should be used by healthcare practitioners.

Another key thing to remember while employing coding modifiers is to follow industry norms. The American Medical Association (AMA) publishes guidelines for the proper use of modifiers, including when each modifier should be used. These rules should be followed by healthcare practitioners to ensure compliance with industry standards.

It is also critical to employ modifiers consistently. In all documentation and billing, healthcare professionals should use the same modifier for the same condition. This helps to assure billing and reimbursement accuracy and consistency.

Modifiers should be used in tandem with the relevant code. Modifiers should be separated by a hyphen and added to the end of the code to which they apply. This ensures that the modifier is paired with the relevant code and situation.

It is critical to avoid the practice of code unbundling. The practice of employing numerous codes to describe a method or service that should be contained under a single, comprehensive code is referred to as unbundling codes. This can result in overbilling and is against industry norms. When possible, healthcare professionals should use comprehensive codes and only use extra codes to convey further information about the treatment or service.

Healthcare practitioners should also refer to approved modifier lists for their specific coding system. The Current Procedural Terminology (CPT) coding system, for example, contains a list of modifiers that can be used to convey further information about a process or service. Only modifiers that are allowed for their coding system should be used by healthcare providers.

Finally, healthcare practitioners should ensure that any modifiers applied are supported by documentation. The documentation should explicitly clarify the circumstances in which the modification was applied, as well as the need for the modifier. This helps to assure billing and reimbursement accuracy and compliance.

Overall, the use of coding modifiers in medical documentation and billing is governed by particular regulations and guidelines. Modifiers should be used by healthcare professionals only when absolutely necessary, in accordance with industry standards, and in conjunction with the appropriate code. They should also avoid the practice of unbundling codes, refer to approved lists of modifiers, and verify that any modifiers used are supported by documentation. By adhering to these laws and norms, healthcare professionals can ensure billing and reimbursement accuracy and compliance, as well as deliver better care to their patients.

Chapter 7: Auditing and Compliance for Medical Coding

- An overview of medical coding auditing and compliance

Medical coding auditing and compliance is a critical component of both healthcare reimbursement and regulatory compliance. The process of assigning number or alphanumeric codes to medical diagnoses and procedures for billing and payment is known as medical coding. Medical coding audits are performed to ensure that medical coding is correct, full, and in accordance with healthcare standards.

Medical coding audits are classified into three types: pre-bill audits, retrospective audits, and focused audits. Pre-bill audits are performed prior to the submission of medical claims to insurance carriers to ensure that the coding is accurate and compliant. After claims have been paid, retrospective audits are performed to check that the coding was correct and that payment was reasonable. Specific sections of code are audited to detect potential compliance concerns or areas for improvement.

Medical coding compliance is critical for ensuring that healthcare practitioners are properly reimbursed for the services they deliver and for remaining in accordance with healthcare legislation. Fines, legal action, and reputational damage can all occur from noncompliance issues.

Medical coding compliance includes several different areas, including documentation, coding accuracy, and compliance with healthcare regulations. Documentation must be accurate, complete, and compliant with healthcare regulations to ensure that the coding is accurate and that reimbursement is appropriate. Coding accuracy is essential to ensure that medical claims are processed correctly and that healthcare providers are reimbursed appropriately. Compliance with healthcare regulations entails following norms and regulations established by government agencies and insurance providers, such as the Centers for Medicare and Medicaid Services (CMS) and the Health Insurance Portability and Accountability Act (HIPAA) (HIPAA).

Medical coding audits can reveal potential compliance issues as well as possibilities for improvement in the coding process. Audits can detect coding flaws, inadequacies in documentation, and possible areas for fraud or misuse. By identifying and addressing these challenges, healthcare providers can enhance the accuracy and compliance of their medical coding procedures.

In conclusion, medical coding auditing and compliance is an essential aspect of healthcare reimbursement and regulatory compliance. Medical coding audits are used to ensure that medical coding is accurate, complete, and compliant with healthcare regulations. Compliance issues can result in fines, legal action, and reputational damage for healthcare providers. Medical coding compliance includes documentation, coding accuracy, and compliance with healthcare regulations. Medical coding audits can identify potential compliance issues and areas for improvement in the medical coding process. By identifying these issues, healthcare providers can take corrective action to improve the accuracy and compliance of their medical coding processes.

– Importance of compliance in medical coding

Medical coding compliance is critical in the healthcare industry. Medical coding is used to document and charge for medical operations and services, and proper coding ensures that healthcare practitioners are properly reimbursed for the services they offer. The use of coding norms and laws guarantees that healthcare providers charge appropriately and ethically.

One reason why medical coding compliance is crucial is to prevent fraud and abuse in the healthcare industry. Fraudulent or abusive billing methods can result in considerable financial penalties as well as legal ramifications for healthcare professionals. Compliance with coding norms and laws aids in ensuring that healthcare professionals charge accurately and ethically, and it can aid in the prevention of fraudulent or abusive billing practices.

Medical coding compliance is also vital for ensuring that patients receive adequate care. Correct coding aids in ensuring that patients receive the proper level of care and are not subjected to needless or inappropriate procedures. Compliance with coding norms and laws aids in ensuring that healthcare practitioners offer high-quality care to their patients while avoiding engaging in inappropriate or unethical behaviors.

Another reason that medical coding compliance is crucial is to guarantee that healthcare practitioners are properly reimbursed for the services they deliver. Accurate coding helps to ensure that healthcare professionals are compensated at the proper rate for the services they deliver and are neither underpaid or overpaid. Compliance with coding norms and laws helps to guarantee that healthcare providers are adequately compensated for their services.

Medical coding compliance is also critical for preserving the healthcare industry's credibility. Accurate and ethical coding methods contribute to the healthcare industry's public and patient trust. Compliance with coding norms and laws helps to guarantee that healthcare providers are honest and dedicated to providing high-quality care to their patients.

Finally, medical coding compliance is critical for ensuring that healthcare providers may function in a financially viable manner. Accurate and ethical coding standards serve to guarantee that healthcare providers are fairly reimbursed for the services they offer and may operate in a financially sustainable way. Compliance with coding norms and laws contributes to healthcare professionals' ability to give high-quality care to their patients in the long run.

Overall, medical coding compliance is critical in the healthcare industry. Compliance with coding guidelines and regulations helps to prevent fraud and abuse, ensures that patients receive appropriate care, that healthcare providers are appropriately reimbursed, that the healthcare industry's integrity is maintained, and that healthcare providers can operate in a financially sustainable manner. Healthcare professionals can assure accurate and ethical billing processes and deliver better treatment to their patients by adhering to coding norms and regulations.

- Different types of medical coding audits

Medical coding audits are an essential part of the revenue cycle management process in healthcare. These audits are conducted to ensure that medical coding is accurate, complete, and compliant with healthcare regulations. There are several different types of medical coding audits that can be conducted, each with its own unique purpose.

1. Pre-bill audits: Pre-bill audits are conducted before medical claims are submitted to insurance providers to ensure that the coding is accurate and compliant. These audits are typically conducted by medical coding specialists or auditors and involve a review of the documentation to ensure that the coding accurately reflects the services provided.

2. Retrospective audits: Retrospective audits are conducted after claims have been paid to ensure that the coding was accurate and that reimbursement was appropriate. These audits are typically conducted by third-party auditors and involve a review of the medical record documentation to ensure that the coding accurately reflects the services provided.

3. Focused audits are performed on specific areas of coding to detect potential compliance concerns or areas for improvement. Internal auditors or third-party auditors may conduct these audits, which can focus on a specific type of service, such as laboratory tests or imaging procedures.

4. Random audits: Random audits are conducted on a random selection of medical claims to ensure that the coding is accurate and compliant. These audits are typically conducted by third-party auditors and can be used to identify potential compliance issues or areas for improvement in the medical coding process.

5. Comparative audits: Comparative audits compare the coding practices of one healthcare provider to those of other providers in the same specialty or

geographic area. These audits can be used to identify potential compliance issues or areas for improvement in the medical coding process.

6. Self-audits: Self-audits are conducted by healthcare providers themselves to ensure that their medical coding is accurate and compliant with healthcare regulations. These audits can be conducted on a regular basis to identify potential compliance issues or areas for improvement in the medical coding process.

In conclusion, medical coding audits are an essential part of the revenue cycle management process in healthcare. There are several different types of medical coding audits that can be conducted, each with its own unique purpose. Pre-bill audits are conducted before medical claims are submitted to insurance providers, retrospective audits are conducted after claims have been paid, focused audits are conducted on specific areas of coding, random audits are conducted on a random selection of medical claims, comparative audits compare the coding practices of one healthcare provider to those of other providers, and self-audits are conducted by healthcare providers themselves. By conducting these audits, healthcare providers can ensure that their medical coding is accurate, complete, and compliant with healthcare regulations.

Chapter 8: Medical Coding Practice Management

- Basics of medical coding practice management

Medical coding practice management is an important aspect of the healthcare sector. Medical coding practice management entails the administration and management of medical records, billing and coding processes, regulatory compliance, and financial elements of medical practice.

The precise and timely documentation of medical records is one of the fundamental concepts of medical coding practice management. Medical records must be thorough and accurate, and they must give a clear and succinct record of the patient's medical history, diagnosis, and treatments. Correct and timely documentation is critical for accurate coding and invoicing, as well as ensuring that patients receive the necessary care.

Compliance with regulatory regulations is another fundamental aspect of medical coding practice management. Healthcare providers must follow a number of rules, including HIPAA laws, Medicare and Medicaid regulations, and others. Compliance with these requirements is critical for safeguarding patient privacy, preventing fraud and abuse, and upholding ethical and legal standards in the healthcare profession.

The correct and ethical coding and billing of medical procedures and services is also part of medical coding practice management. Healthcare providers must utilize accurate and appropriate codes for the treatments and services they

43

offer, and they must bill for those services accordingly. Ethical coding and billing methods aid in ensuring that healthcare practitioners are fairly compensated for the services they offer and that patients receive high-quality treatment.

Effective medical coding practice management also includes financial aspects of medical practice management. Healthcare providers must properly manage their finances, which includes budgeting, cash flow management, and financial reporting. Effective financial management ensures the long-term viability of medical practices and allows healthcare providers to provide high-quality treatment to their patients.

Finally, medical coding practice management entails human and resource management. Healthcare providers must efficiently manage their workers, including hiring, training, and managing employees. Personnel management that is effective helps to guarantee that healthcare practitioners have the resources they need to offer high-quality treatment to their patients.

In conclusion, medical coding practice management is an important aspect of the healthcare sector. It entails the administration and management of medical records, regulatory compliance, accurate and ethical coding and billing methods, financial management, and people and resource management. Healthcare providers can guarantee that they are giving high-quality care to their patients, operating ethically and legally, and managing their resources effectively by adhering to basic principles of medical coding practice management.

- Billing and reimbursement for medical coding

Medical billing and reimbursement are key components of healthcare revenue cycle management. The process of assigning number or alphanumeric codes to medical diagnoses and procedures for billing and payment is known as medical coding. Medical coding is used to create medical claims, which are then submitted to insurance companies for compensation for medical services supplied to patients.

Medical billing is the process of filing medical claims for reimbursement to insurance companies. The collecting of patient information, including insurance and demographic information, is the first step in the medical billing process. Medical coders assign codes to medical treatments and services after collecting patient information. The medical claims are subsequently submitted for reimbursement to insurance companies.

The process of getting payment from insurance providers for medical services supplied to patients is known as reimbursement. The categorization of medical procedures and services supplied is often used to determine reimbursement. Insurance companies utilize reimbursement rates to calculate how much money healthcare providers will receive for medical services rendered.

In healthcare, there are various distinct types of reimbursement schemes. Fee-for-service payment is a typical way of reimbursing healthcare professionals for each medical treatment given. Capitation reimbursement is a system of payment in which healthcare professionals are paid a set sum per patient per month, regardless of the number of medical services delivered. Bundled payment reimbursement is a reimbursement technique in which a predetermined amount is paid to a healthcare practitioner for a group of connected medical services supplied to a patient.

Medical billing and reimbursement are governed by healthcare legislation such as HIPAA and CMS rules. To prevent fines, legal action, and reputational damage, healthcare providers must verify that their medical coding and billing processes are in accordance with these standards. Accurate and thorough documentation, coding accuracy, and reimbursement rules all contribute to compliance with healthcare regulations.

Medical coding billing and reimbursement practices that are effective are critical for healthcare providers to retain financial viability while providing high-quality patient care. To assist with medical coding billing and payment, healthcare practitioners can employ technology such as electronic health record (EHR) systems and coding software. To guarantee compliance with healthcare legislation, healthcare providers should also ensure that their staff employees, especially medical coders and other administrative staff, undergo regular training and education on medical coding billing and payment processes.

Finally, medical coding billing and reimbursement is an essential component of healthcare revenue cycle management. Medical coding is used to create medical claims that are submitted to insurance companies for reimbursement. The categorization of medical procedures and services supplied is often used to determine reimbursement. Medical coding billing and reimbursement practices that are effective are critical for healthcare providers to retain financial viability while providing high-quality patient care. Compliance with healthcare standards, including accurate and full documentation, coding accuracy, and reimbursement rules compliance, is critical to prevent penalties, legal action, and reputational damage. Healthcare practitioners can employ technology, as well as training and education, to help with medical coding, billing, and reimbursement methods, as well as to maintain compliance with healthcare legislation.

– Medical coding software and technology

Medical coding software and technology have become an essential component of the healthcare industry. Medical coding software and technology are used to streamline medical coding and billing processes, improve accuracy and efficiency, and provide healthcare providers with the tools they need to manage their practices effectively.

One of the most important benefits of medical coding software and technology is improved accuracy and efficiency. Medical coding software and technology can help healthcare providers to accurately code and bill for medical procedures and services, reducing the risk of errors and improving the overall efficiency of the billing process. This can help healthcare providers to save time and resources, and focus on providing high-quality care to their patients.

Another important benefit of medical coding software and technology is the ability to manage medical records more effectively. Medical coding software and technology can help healthcare providers to organize and manage medical records more effectively, making it easier to access and share patient information. Medical coding software and technology can also help to improve compliance with regulatory requirements. Healthcare providers must comply with a variety of regulations, including HIPAA regulations, Medicare and Medicaid regulations, and other regulatory requirements. Medical coding software and technology can help healthcare providers to track and manage compliance with these regulations, reducing the risk of non-compliance and the associated penalties.

Another benefit of medical coding software and technology is the ability to track and manage financial aspects of medical practice more effectively. Medical coding software and technology can help healthcare providers to manage their finances more effectively, including budgeting, cash flow management, and financial reporting. This can help healthcare providers to make informed financial decisions, and ensure the sustainability of their practices over the long term.

Finally, medical coding software and technology can help healthcare providers to improve patient outcomes. By providing healthcare providers with access to accurate and up-to-date medical records, medical coding software and technology can help to improve the quality of care provided to patients. This can help to reduce the risk of medical errors, improve patient satisfaction, and ultimately improve patient outcomes.

In summary, medical coding software and technology have become essential tools for healthcare providers. They help to streamline medical coding and billing processes, improve accuracy and efficiency, manage medical records more effectively, improve compliance with regulatory requirements, track and manage financial aspects of medical practice, and improve patient outcomes. By leveraging the benefits of medical coding software and technology, healthcare providers can improve the quality of care they provide to their patients, while also managing their practices more effectively.

300 Possible questions and answers for the CPC exam

1. What does medical coding serve?

To correctly identify and record medical treatments and services for billing and reimbursement purposes, that's the objective of medical coding.

2. What distinguishes ICD-10-CM from ICD-10-PCS?

ICD-10-PCS is used to code operations, whereas ICD-10-CM is used to code diagnoses.

3. What distinguishes HCPCS codes from CPT codes?

In response, medical equipment, supplies, and other non-physician services are coded using HCPCS numbers whereas medical operations and services are coded using CPT codes.

4. What does medical coding unbundling entail?

In place of using a single comprehensive code for the entire treatment, unbundling is the practice of invoicing different codes for different parts of a same procedure.

5. What does medical coding upcoding entail?

In order to improve compensation, upcoding is the practice of utilizing a higher-level code than is necessary.

6. What is the main purpose of the National Correct Coding Initiative (NCCI)?

The National Correct Coding Initiative promotes proper coding practices and reduces erroneous payments.

7. How do main and secondary diagnoses differ from one another?

A secondary diagnosis is a condition that is not the major reason for the visit but may have an impact on the patient's management or treatment. A primary diagnosis is the main cause for the patient's visit.

8. How do you distinguish between a symptom and a sign?

A sign is a physical indication of a medical condition, whereas a symptom is a patient-reported subjective sign of a medical condition.

9. What distinguishes an add-on code from a modifier?

An add-on code is an additional code used to record an additional service or process done during the same session, whereas a modifier code is used to indicate that a service or operation was modified in some way.

10. What distinguishes a follow-up phase from a global period?

A follow-up period is a time frame in which further services or procedures may be required to manage the patient's condition, as opposed to a global term, during which all associated services and procedures are covered by the payment for a particular procedure.

11. What distinguishes a claim from an encounter?

An encounter is a particular instance of a patient receiving medical care, whereas a claim is a request for reimbursement for services given.

12. What distinguishes a preauthorization from a pre-certification?

Pre-certification is the process by which a healthcare provider confirms that a specific service or procedure is covered by the patient's insurance plan, whereas pre-authorization is the process by which a healthcare provider requests approval from a payer before providing a specific service or procedure.

13. What distinguishes a contemporaneous review from a retrospective review?

The difference between a contemporaneous review and a retrospective review is that a concurrent review looks at medical records and claims while the patient is still receiving treatment.

14. What is the difference between a remittance advisory remark code and a claim adjustment reason code?

Claim adjustment reason codes are used to show why a claim was changed, whereas remittance advice remark codes are used to give specifics about changes.

15. What is the difference between a medical rationale and a medical necessity?

Medical necessity, as opposed to medical rationale, which explains why a certain service or operation is required for a specific patient, is the requirement that a service or procedure is required for the diagnosis or treatment of a medical condition.

16. What distinguishes covered services from uninsured services?

A service is considered covered if it can be reimbursed by a patient's insurance plan, and it is considered non-covered if it cannot.

17. What are the differences between benefit periods and calendar years?

A benefit period, as opposed to a calendar year, which is a twelve-month period beginning on January 1st, is the length of time during which a patient is entitled for benefits under their insurance plan.

18. What distinguishes a charge master from a fee schedule?

A charge master is a list of the fees for all services and procedures rendered by a healthcare provider, whereas a fee schedule is a list of approved fees for certain medical treatments and procedures.

19. What distinguishes a copayment from a coinsurance?

Coinsurance is a proportion of the total cost of services that the patient is responsible for paying, whereas a copayment is a fixed sum paid by the patient at the time of service.

20. What is the difference between a value-based payment approach and a fee-for-service payment model?

A value-based payment model compensates healthcare professionals based on the effectiveness and efficiency of the treatment they provide, as opposed to a fee-for-service payment model that compensates them for each service or procedure given.

21. What distinguishes a prospective denial from a retroactive denial?

A prospective denial is a refusal to pay for services that have not yet been rendered, as opposed to a retroactive denial, which refuses to pay for services that have already been rendered.

22. What distinguishes a medical review from a utilization review?

While a utilization review examines medical records and claims to make sure that services and procedures are being used properly and effectively, a medical review examines medical records and claims to make sure that they are medically required and acceptable.

23. What differentiates a DRG from an APC?

APC (Ambulatory Payment Classification) is a system for grouping outpatient services and procedures based on similar clinical characteristics and resource utilization, whereas DRG (Diagnosis-Related Group) is a system for grouping inpatient hospital stays based on similar diagnoses and treatments.

24. What distinguishes a RAC audit from a MAC audit?

In contrast to MAC (Medicare Administrative Contractor) audit, which examines claims for conformity with Medicare rules and regulations, RAC (Recovery Audit Contractor) audit examines claims for erroneous payments.

25. What distinguishes an E/M code from a surgical code?

The correct answer is that office visits and other non-surgical services are coded using E/M (Evaluation and Management) codes, whereas procedures and operations are coded using surgical codes.

26. What distinguishes a quality assurance program from a compliance program?

In contrast to a quality assurance program, which is intended to guarantee that healthcare providers are delivering high-quality care, a compliance program is one that checks that healthcare providers are adhering to ethical and regulatory requirements.

27. What distinguishes a claim scrubber from a claim edit?

A claim scrubber is a piece of software used to fix coding flaws and inconsistencies in claims, as opposed to a claim edit, which is a software application intended to spot them.

28. What distinguishes a surgical assistant package from a global surgical package?

In contrast to a surgical assistant package, which only contains services and procedures given by a surgical assistant, a global surgical package covers all services and procedures associated with an operation.

29. What distinguishes a facility claim from a professional claim?

In contrast to facility claims, which are claims for services rendered by healthcare facilities like hospitals or clinics, professional claims are those for services rendered by healthcare professionals like doctors or nurse practitioners.

30. What distinguishes a benefit explanation from a remittance advice?

A remittance advice is a letter delivered to healthcare providers outlining the amount of reimbursement they will get for services rendered, whereas an explanation of benefits is a letter sent to patients outlining the amount of reimbursement their insurer will offer for services received.

31. What distinguishes an observation stay from an inpatient admission?

A hospital stay of at least one night is considered an inpatient admission, whereas a shorter stay for monitoring and testing is considered an observation stay.

32. What makes a modifier 25 different from a modifier 59?

While modification 59 indicates that a service was different or independent of other services provided during the same contact, modifier 25 indicates that a separately identifiable service was provided inside the same encounter.

33. What distinguishes a consultation visit from a follow-up visit?

A follow-up visit is one where a healthcare professional monitors and maintains an ongoing medical condition, whereas a consultative visit is one where a healthcare provider offers an expert opinion or advise on a particular medical issue.

34. What distinguishes an ABN from an HINN, number 34?

The difference between an ABN (Advance Beneficiary Notice) and an HINN (Hospital Issued Notice of Noncoverage) is that the former is given to a patient prior to a service or procedure that might not be covered by their insurance, while the latter is given to a patient prior to a hospital stay that might not be covered by their insurance.

35. What distinguishes a pathology laboratory from a clinical laboratory?

In contrast to a pathology laboratory, which conducts testing on tissue samples and other biological specimens, a clinical laboratory conducts tests on blood, urine, and other bodily fluids.

36. What distinguishes a diagnostic test from a screening test?

A diagnostic test is used to confirm or rule out a medical problem in a particular person, whereas a screening test is designed to discover people who may have a medical condition.

37. What makes a face-to-face consultation different from a telemedicine consultation?

A face-to-face encounter occurs when a patient and a healthcare provider meet in person, whereas a telemedicine encounter occurs when a patient and a healthcare provider meet digitally, such as via video conferencing.

38. What distinguishes a medical appropriateness from a medical necessity?

In contrast to medical appropriateness, which is defined as a service or process that complies with current medical standards and is likely to benefit the patient, medical necessity refers to a service or procedure that is necessary to diagnose or treat a medical condition.

39. What is the difference between a privacy plan and a compliance strategy?

While a privacy strategy is designed to keep patient information private and secure, a compliance plan is designed to guarantee that healthcare providers follow regulatory requirements.

40. What distinguishes a billing system from a code set?

A billing system is a software system used to create and submit claims for payment, whereas a code set is a standard list of codes used to identify medical operations, diagnoses, and other healthcare services.

41. How do a claim and a bill differ from one another?

A claim is a request for compensation for services received, whereas a bill is a breakdown of the costs associated with such services.

42. What distinguishes a primary payer from a secondary payer?

A secondary payer is an insurance plan that might offer additional coverage for the same claim, whereas a primary payer is the insurance plan that pays out claims first.

43. What distinguishes a utilization review from a medical necessity evaluation?

An evaluation of a service or procedure's medical need is known as a medical necessity review. In contrast, an evaluation of a service or procedure's utilization is known as a utilization review.

44. What distinguishes a contemporaneous review from a retrospective review?

The difference between a contemporaneous review and a retrospective review is that a concurrent review looks at medical records and claims while the patient is still receiving treatment.

45. What distinguishes a screening test from a diagnostic test?

A screening test is used to identify a medical issue in people who may not be displaying any symptoms, as opposed to a diagnostic test, which is used to confirm or rule out a suspected medical condition.

46. What differentiates a general practitioner from a specialist?

In contrast to a primary care physician, who provides basic medical treatment to patients, a specialist is a healthcare worker who has considerable training and experience in a certain field of medicine.

47. What distinguishes a copayment from a deductible?

The difference between a copayment and a deductible is the amount that must be paid out of pocket by the patient prior to the start of insurance coverage.

48. What distinguishes a prospective denial from a retrospective denial?

A prospective denial is a refusal to pay for services that have not yet been rendered, as opposed to a retroactive denial, which refuses payment for services that have already been rendered.

49. What distinguishes a capitation payment scheme from a fee-for-service payment approach?

A capitation payment model pays healthcare providers a fixed sum per patient every month regardless of the services rendered, as opposed to a fee-for-service payment model, which pays healthcare providers for each treatment or procedure rendered.

50. What distinguishes a medical need from a medical judgment call?

Answer: Medical decision-making refers to the process of making clinical decisions based on the patient's medical history, physical examination, and other factors. Medical necessity refers to the requirement that a service or procedure is necessary for the diagnosis or treatment of a medical ailment.

51. What distinguishes a pharmacy from a provider of durable medical equipment (DME)?

The difference between a pharmacy and a DME supplier is that the latter sells drugs and other associated goods while the former sells medical equipment and supplies needed to treat or manage medical problems.

52. What distinguishes a prescription medication from an over-the-counter medication?

An over-the-counter drug can be acquired without a prescription, but a prescription drug can only be obtained with a prescription from a healthcare professional.

53. What is the difference between a health record and a medical record?

A health record is a comprehensive record of a patient's health information, comprising medical data from several providers and facilities, whereas a medical record is a record of a patient's medical history and treatment provided by a single healthcare provider or facility.

54. What is the difference between a durable power of attorney and a healthcare proxy?

A durable power of attorney, on the other hand, appoints someone to make financial and legal choices on another person's behalf. A healthcare proxy, on the other hand, appoints someone to make medical choices on behalf of another person who is unable to do so themselves.

55. What distinguishes a living will from a healthcare directive?

A living will is a particular kind of healthcare directive that specifies a person's preferences for end-of-life care. A healthcare directive is a legal document that explains a person's wishes for medical treatment in the event that they are unable to make decisions for themselves.

56. What distinguishes an observational study from a clinical trial?

In contrast to an observational study, which involves just observing individuals and gathering data without assigning them to receive any particular treatment or intervention, a clinical trial involves assigning participants to receive a specific therapy or intervention.

57. What distinguishes a hospitalist from a primary care physician?

In contrast to primary care physicians, who treat patients on an outpatient basis, hospitalists are healthcare professionals who specialize in the treatment of hospitalized patients.

58. What distinguishes an emergency department from an urgent care facility?

An emergency department treats patients who have life-threatening illnesses and other emergencies, whereas an urgent care center treats non-life-threatening ailments on a walk-in basis.

59. What distinguishes a medical examiner from a coroner?

While a coroner is an elected person who investigates deaths and may or may not have medical training, a medical examiner does autopsies and establishes the cause of death in circumstances when it is ambiguous.

60. What makes a brand-name medication different from a generic medication?

A brand-name drug is one that is marketed under a specific brand name, whereas a generic drug has the same active ingredient as a brand-name drug and is equivalent in terms of safety, dose, and effectiveness.

61. What distinguishes an inpatient procedure from an outpatient one?

An inpatient procedure is one that necessitates a hospital stay, whereas an outpatient operation can be carried out in a clinic or other healthcare facility without necessitating a hospital stay.

62. What distinguishes a nurse from a medical assistant?

A nurse is a healthcare professional who offers direct patient care and may have advanced training and specialization, whereas a medical assistant is a healthcare professional that works administrative and clinical activities under the supervision of a doctor or nurse.

63. How do a personal care assistant and a home health aide differ from one another?

A home health aide provides medical and personal care services to those who are recovering from an illness or accident, whereas a personal care assistant assists people who require help with activities of daily living like washing and dressing due to disease or disability.

64. What is the difference between a psychiatrist and a mental health counselor?

A psychiatrist is a medical practitioner who specializes in the diagnosis and treatment of mental health issues and can prescribe medication, whereas a mental health counselor is a healthcare professional who provides counseling and therapy to those suffering from mental illnesses.

65. What is the difference between a nursing home and an assisted living facility?

A nursing home provides 24-hour medical care and daily living assistance to persons who require more intensive care, whereas an assisted living facility provides accommodation, meals, and daily living assistance to people who need some assistance but do not require 24-hour medical care.

66. What distinguishes a translator from a medical interpreter?

In contrast to a translator, who translates written material from one language into another, a medical interpreter is a trained specialist who helps healthcare personnel and patients who speak various languages communicate.

67. What is the difference between a flexible spending account (FSA) and a health savings account (HSA)?

An FSA is a tax-advantaged account that can be used to pay for qualified medical expenses; however, funds must be used by the end of the fiscal year or they will be forfeited. A health savings account (HSA) is a tax-advantaged savings account that can be used to pay for eligible medical costs.

68. What distinguishes a clinical trial from a medical research study?

A clinical trial is a research study in which participants are assigned to receive a particular therapy or intervention, whereas a medical research study is one done to acquire information regarding a medical condition, treatment, or intervention.

69. What distinguishes a hospital board of directors from a medical ethics committee?

A hospital board of directors is a group of people who manage a hospital's entire operations, including financial and strategic decisions. A medical ethics committee is a group of healthcare professionals that study and make judgments regarding ethical issues relating to patient care.

70. What distinguishes a personal trainer from a health coach?

While a personal trainer is a fitness expert who creates and oversees exercise programs to help people improve their physical fitness, a health coach is a healthcare professional who assists people in setting and achieving health goals and making lifestyle adjustments.

71. What is the difference between an electronic health record (EHR) and a health information exchange (HIE)?

An electronic health record is a digital record of a patient's health information kept by a single healthcare provider or facility, whereas a health information exchange is a system that allows numerous healthcare providers to exchange patient information electronically.

72. What distinguishes a medical error from a medical malpractice?

Medical malpractice is a legal claim brought by a patient who has been damaged by a healthcare professional's negligent or purposeful conduct, as opposed to a medical error, which is a mistake made by a healthcare provider that causes injury to a patient.

73. What distinguishes a medical discharge from a medical clearance?

A medical release is a document signed by a healthcare professional that permits a patient to engage in a specific activity or return to work following an illness or injury, whereas a medical clearance is a process in which a healthcare provider evaluates a patient's health to determine if they are medically fit for a specific activity or procedure.

74. What distinguishes a medical certificate from a medical license?

A medical license is a legal document that confirms a healthcare provider's ability to practice medicine in a certain jurisdiction, whereas a medical certificate certifies a person's fitness for a particular activity or job.

75. What distinguishes a medical exemption from a medical waiver?

A medical waiver releases a person from a legal obligation owing to a medical condition, whereas a medical exemption grants a person a waiver from a vaccination requirement due to a medical condition.

76. What distinguishes a medical ID card from a medical alert bracelet?

A medical ID card is a card that contains details on a person's medical history and is kept in a wallet or purse, whereas a medical alert bracelet is a band worn by a person with a medical condition or allergy to alert others in case of an emergency.

77. What distinguishes a medical claim from a health insurance claim?

A health insurance claim is a request from an insurance provider for reimbursement for medical services received, whereas a medical claim is a request for payment for medical services provided.

78. What is the difference between a medical retirement and a medical discharge?

A medical retirement differs from a medical discharge in that the latter relates to the decision to leave the military due to a medical condition.

79. What distinguishes a medical transfer from an emergency medical evacuation?

A medical transport is the movement of a patient from one medical institution to another for specialized treatment or care, whereas a medical evacuation is the movement of a patient from a remote or hazardous place to a medical facility for treatment.

80. What distinguishes a medical release from a medical waiver?

A medical release is a document signed by a healthcare provider that permits a patient to engage in a certain activity or return to work following an illness or accident, whereas a medical waiver exempts a person from a legal requirement due to a medical condition.

81. What distinguishes a personal emergency response system from a medical alert system?

A personal emergency response system is a device installed in a home that can be used to call for help in the case of an emergency, whereas a medical alert system is a device worn by a person that may be used to call for help in the event of a medical emergency.

82. What distinguishes a medical examiner from a forensic pathologist?

A medical examiner is a medical practitioner who performs autopsies and establishes the cause of death in uncertain instances, whereas a forensic pathologist is a medical doctor who specializes in the investigation of deaths and injuries that may be tied to criminal behavior.

83. What is the distinction between a medical device and a pharmaceutical?

A medical device is used to diagnose, treat, or prevent a medical ailment or illness, whereas a pharmaceutical product is used to treat or manage a medical condition or disease.

84. How is a medical procedure different from a surgical operation?

A medical procedure is conducted by a healthcare provider in order to diagnose or treat a medical ailment or disease, whereas a surgical operation includes cutting into the body in order to treat a medical condition or disease.

85. What is the distinction between a medical diagnostic and a prognosis?

A medical prognosis is a forecast of the expected course and outcome of a medical ailment or disease.

86. What is the distinction between a medical treatment and an intervention?

A medical intervention is any activity taken to treat a medical ailment or disease, including treatments, procedures, and surgeries.

87. What is the difference between a medical history and a medical record?

A medical record is a detailed record of a patient's health information, including medical history, current symptoms, and treatment provided by a particular healthcare provider or facility.

88. What is the distinction between a living will and a health care directive?

A living will is a type of medical directive that specifies a person's preferences for end-of-life care.

89. How does a medical coder differ from a medical transcriptionist?

A medical transcriptionist is a healthcare professional who transcribes medical records, whereas a medical coder assigns billing and insurance codes to medical data.

90. How does a therapy dog vary from a medical alert dog?

A therapy dog is a dog that has been trained to bring comfort and companionship to people in hospitals, nursing homes, and other healthcare facilities. A medical alert dog is a properly trained canine that can detect changes in a person's body odor or behavior and notify them to a potentially dangerous medical condition or emergency.

What's the distinction between a coroner and a medical examiner?

A medical examiner is a medical doctor who performs autopsies and determines the cause of death in cases when the cause of death is unknown, whereas a coroner is an elected official who investigates deaths and may or may not have medical expertise.

92. What is the difference between a medical laboratory technician and a medical laboratory scientist?

A medical laboratory technician performs routine laboratory tests and processes, whereas a medical laboratory scientist performs more complex laboratory tests and procedures and may be involved in research and the development of novel laboratory tests.

93. How can you tell the difference between a medical alert tag and a medical identification bracelet?

A medical alert tag is a small metal tag that may be connected to a keychain or other personal item that carries information about a person's medical condition or allergies. A medical ID bracelet, on the other hand, is a bracelet worn by an individual that provides information about a person's medical condition or allergy.

94. What is the distinction between a medical aide and a medical scribe?

A medical scribe records real-time patient contacts while a physician provides care, whereas a medical assistant performs administrative and clinical tasks under the supervision of a physician or nurse.

95. How does a forensic psychologist vary from a medical examiner?

A forensic psychologist applies psychological principles to legal matters such as criminal investigations and trials, whereas a medical examiner performs autopsies and determines the cause of death in ambiguous cases.

96. How does a fall detection system vary from a medical alert system?

A medical alert system is a device that a person wears that can be used to call for help in the event of a medical emergency, whereas a fall detection system utilizes sensors to detect when a person falls and automatically calls for help if the user is unable to do so themselves.

97. What is the distinction between a medical malpractice and a medical negligence claim?

A medical malpractice claim is brought against a healthcare professional when an act or omission falls below the established standard of care and causes injury or harm to a patient. A medical negligence claim, on the other hand, is filed against a healthcare professional for failing to satisfy the standard of care, but it does not always result in injury or harm.

98. What distinguishes a medical alert pendant from a medical alert button?

A medical alert pendant is a device worn around the neck that calls for assistance in the case of a medical emergency, whereas a medical alert button is a device worn on the wrist or placed in a convenient location that calls for assistance in the event of a medical emergency.

99. What is the difference between a medical translator and an interpreter?

A medical interpreter provides interpretation services to patients and healthcare staff who speak different languages, whereas a medical translator provides textual translation services for medical records and information.

100. What is the difference between a durable and a medical power of attorney?

A medical power of attorney is a legal document that appoints someone to make medical decisions for someone else if they are unable to do so themselves, whereas a durable power of attorney appoints someone to make financial and legal decisions for someone else, including if they become incapacitated.

101. What is the main difference between a medical certificate and a medical clearance?

A medical certificate certifies a person's fitness to perform a specific task, such as flying an airplane or operating heavy machinery, whereas a medical clearance certifies a person's overall health and ability to participate in physical activities.

102. What is the difference between a medical and a physical examination?

A medical exam is a thorough examination that includes medical tests and evaluations, whereas a physical exam is a routine check performed by a healthcare provider to assess an individual's overall health.

103. What distinguishes a medical alert necklace from a medical alert bracelet?

A medical alert necklace is a device worn around the neck that is used to summon assistance in the event of a medical emergency, whereas a medical alert bracelet is a device worn on the wrist that is used to summon assistance in the event of a medical emergency.

104. How do you tell the difference between a medical diagnosis and a medical evaluation?

A medical diagnosis is the identification of the underlying cause of a medical condition or disease, whereas a medical assessment is a comprehensive assessment of an individual's overall health.

105. What is the distinction between a medical discharge and a medical retirement?

A medical discharge is a type of military discharge granted to service members who are unable to continue serving due to a medical condition, whereas a medical retirement is a type of military retirement granted to service members who are unable to continue serving due to a medical condition and have served for a certain period of time.

106. What distinguishes a medical alert pendant from a medical alert watch?

A medical alert pendant is a device worn around the neck that calls for assistance in the case of a medical emergency, whereas a medical alert watch is a device worn on the wrist that calls for assistance in the event of a medical emergency.

107. How does a forensic scientist vary from a medical examiner?

A medical examiner is a doctor who performs autopsies and determines the cause of death in cases when the cause of death is unknown, whereas a forensic scientist analyzes physical evidence in criminal investigations.

108. What is the difference between a medical alert system and a medical monitoring system?

A medical alert system is a device that a person wears to call for help in the event of a medical emergency, whereas a medical monitoring system is a device that monitors a person's vital signs and health status.

109. What is the difference between a medical alert bracelet and a medical ID tag?

A medical alert bracelet is a wristband that contains information about a person's medical condition or allergies, whereas a medical ID tag is a small metal tag attached to a keychain or other personal object that contains the same information.

110. What is the difference between a medical device and a piece of medical equipment?

The instruments and equipment used by healthcare personnel to diagnose, treat, and monitor patients are referred to as medical equipment.

111. What distinguishes a medical alert system from a personal safety device?

A medical alert system is a device that a person wears that can be used to summon aid in the event of a medical emergency, whereas a personal safety device is a gadget that alerts people to an emergency or danger.

112. What is the difference between a medical examiner and a coroner's assistant?

A medical examiner is a doctor who performs autopsies and determines the cause of death in cases when the cause of death is unknown, whereas a coroner's assistant is a professional who assists the coroner in investigating deaths.

113. What's the distinction between a GPS tracker and a medical alert system?

A GPS tracker is a device that tracks a person's or object's location. A medical alert system is a device worn by a person that can be used to request assistance in the event of a medical emergency.

114. What is the difference between a medical alert system and a panic button?

A medical alert system is a device that an individual wears that can be used to summon help in the event of a medical emergency, whereas a panic button is a device that may be used to summon help in the event of an emergency or danger.

115. How does a personal emergency response system differ from a medical alert system?

A personal emergency response system is a device installed in a home that can be used to call for help in the case of an emergency, whereas a medical alert system is a device worn by a person that may be used to call for help in the event of a medical emergency.

116. How does a fall prevention system vary from a medical alert system?

A fall prevention system is a device or set of procedures designed to reduce the risk of falls and injury in older people or people with limited mobility.

117. What's the distinction between a healthcare proxy and a medical directive?

A healthcare proxy is a legal document that appoints someone to make medical decisions for another person if they are unable to do so themselves.

118. What is the difference between a medical alert system and a medication reminder system?

A medication reminder system is a device or service that alerts users when it is time to take their medications.

119. How do you tell the difference between a medical diagnosis and a medical evaluation?

A medical diagnosis is the identification of the underlying cause of a medical condition or disease, whereas a medical assessment is a comprehensive review of an individual's overall health, including medical history, physical examination, and diagnostic tests.

120. What is the difference between a medical alert system and a medication dispenser?

A medical alert system is a wearable device that can be used to summon assistance in the event of a medical emergency, whereas a medicine dispenser is a device that distributes medications at the appropriate time and dose.

121. How does a home security system differ from a medical alert system?

A medical alert system is a device that a person wears to call for help in the event of a medical emergency, whereas a home security system is a device or collection of devices that protects a home from burglary and other criminal activity.

122. What is the difference between a medical alert system and a personal safety app?

A personal safety app is a mobile application that can be used to notify others in the event of an emergency or danger, whereas a medical alert system is a device worn by an individual that can be used to ask for assistance in the event of a medical emergency.

123. What's the difference between a medical alert system and a smoke alarm?

A medical alert system is a device that an individual wears to call for help in the event of a medical emergency, whereas a smoke detector detects smoke and alerts building occupants in the event of a fire.

124. What distinguishes a medical alert system from a heart rate monitor?

A heart rate monitor is a device that measures an individual's heart rate and monitors their cardiovascular health, whereas a medical alert system is a gadget that an individual wears and can be used to summon help in the event of a medical emergency.

125. What distinguishes a medical alert system from a blood pressure monitor?

A medical alert system is a device worn by an individual that can be used to summon help in the event of a medical emergency, whereas a blood pressure monitor measures blood pressure and monitors cardiovascular health.

126. How does a personal alarm vary from a medical alert system?

A personal alarm is a device used to seek help in the event of an emergency or danger, whereas a medical alert system is a device worn by an individual that can be used to summon aid in the event of a medical emergency.

127. What is the difference between a medical alert system and a wearable health tracker?

A wearable health tracker is a device that is worn on the body and monitors and tracks health indicators such as heart rate, activity level, and sleep. A medical alert system, on the other hand, is a device worn by an individual that can be used to request assistance in the event of a medical emergency.

128. What's the distinction between a personal fall detection device and a medical alert system?

A personal fall detection device is a device worn on the body that detects falls and warns emergency services in the case of a fall, whereas a medical alert system is a device worn by an individual that can be used to seek for aid in the event of a medical emergency.

129. How does a GPS emergency locator vary from a medical alert system?

A GPS emergency locator is a gadget that can pinpoint the position of a person or object in an emergency. A medical alert system is a device worn by a person that can be used to request assistance in the event of a medical emergency.

130. What is the distinction between a personal panic alarm and a medical alert system?

A personal panic alarm is a device used to seek help in the event of an emergency or danger, whereas a medical alert system is a device worn by an individual that can be used to summon aid in the event of a medical emergency.

131. What makes a personal safety whistle different from a medical alert system?

A personal safety whistle is a device meant to attract attention and summon aid in the event of an emergency or danger, whereas a medical alert system is a device worn by an individual that can be used to summon assistance in the event of a medical emergency.

132. How does a personal safety keychain vary from a medical alert system?

A personal safety keychain is a device attached to a keychain that may be used to call for help in the event of an emergency or danger, whereas a medical alert system is a device worn by an individual that can be used to call for aid in the event of a medical emergency.

133. How does a personal safety horn vary from a medical alert system?

A personal safety horn is a device meant to draw attention and summon aid in the event of an emergency or danger, whereas a medical alert system is a device worn by an individual that can be used to request assistance in the event of a medical emergency.

134. What is the difference between a medical alert system and a personal safety whistle with an integrated flashlight?

A medical alert system is a device worn by a person that can be used to summon assistance in the event of a medical emergency. A personal safety whistle with a built-in flashlight, on the other hand, is a device designed to draw attention and cry for aid in the event of an emergency or danger, and it also has a spotlight for greater visibility in low light settings.

135. How does a personal safety light vary from a medical alert system?

A personal safety light is a gadget meant to increase visibility and make individuals more visible in low-light conditions to prevent accidents or danger. A medical alert system is a device worn by an individual that can be used to seek for assistance in the event of a medical emergency.

136. What is the difference between a medical alert system and a personal safety alarm with an integrated strobe light?

A medical alert system is a device worn by a person that can be used to summon assistance in the event of a medical emergency. A personal safety alarm with a built-in strobe light is a device designed to draw attention and summon assistance in the event of an emergency or danger, and it incorporates a strobe light for improved visibility.

137. What is the distinction between a medical alert system and a personal safety app that is location-based?

A medical alert system is a device worn by an individual that can be used to summon assistance in the event of a medical emergency, whereas a personal safety app with location tracking is an app installed on a mobile device that can be used to alert others in the event of an emergency or danger, and also includes location tracking to assist responders in locating the individual in need.

138. What is the distinction between a medical alert system and a keychain with pepper spray for personal protection?

A medical alert system is a device worn by a person that can be used to summon assistance in the event of a medical emergency. A personal safety keychain with pepper spray, on the other hand, is a gadget intended to defend oneself in the event of an assault or danger, and it comes with a keychain for added convenience.

139. What is the difference between a medical alert system and a personal safety whistle with an integrated compass?

A medical alert system is a device worn by a person that can be used to summon assistance in the event of a medical emergency. A personal safety whistle with a built-in compass, on the other hand, is a device meant to draw attention and cry for aid in the event of an emergency or danger, and it also incorporates a compass for further navigational assistance.

140. What is the difference between a medical alert system and a personal safety device with an integrated camera?

A medical alert system is a device that a person wears to summon assistance in the event of a medical emergency, whereas a personal safety device with a built-in camera is used to record video and gather evidence in the event of an emergency or danger.

141. What's the distinction between a smartwatch and a medical alert system?

A medical alert system is a wearable device that can be used to summon assistance in the event of a medical emergency, whereas a smartwatch is a wearable device that can perform a variety of purposes, including assessing health and sending smartphone notifications.

142. What is the difference between a medical alert system and a panic button?

A medical alert system is a device that an individual wears that can be used to summon help in the event of a medical emergency, whereas a panic button is a device that may be used to summon help in the event of an emergency or danger.

143. What distinguishes a medical alert system from a personal safety app with a panic button?

A medical alert system is a wearable device that may be used to summon assistance in the case of a medical emergency, whereas a personal safety app with a panic button function is an app that can be installed on a mobile device and used to summon assistance in the event of an emergency or danger.

144. What is the difference between a medical alert system and a personal safety app that includes GPS tracking?

A medical alert system is a device worn by an individual that can be used to summon assistance in the event of a medical emergency, whereas a personal safety app with GPS tracking is an application installed on a mobile device that can track the user's location in the event of an emergency or danger.

145. What is the difference between a medical alert system and a personal safety app with a message function?

A personal safety app with a messaging feature is a mobile application that can be used to send messages to pre-selected contacts or emergency services in the event of an emergency or danger. A medical alert system is a device worn by an individual that can be used to call for help in the event of a medical emergency.

146. What is the difference between a medical alert system and a personal safety software that includes a prank call feature?

A personal safety app with a fake call function is an app that can be downloaded into a mobile device and used to imitate a phone call in order to deter potential attackers or provide an excuse to flee a dangerous situation.

147. How does a medical alert system differ from a personal safety app with live streaming capabilities?

A personal safety app with a live streaming function is an application that can send live video and audio to pre-selected contacts or emergency services in the case of an emergency or danger.

148. What distinguishes a medical alert system from a personal safety app with voice recognition?

A medical alert system is a device worn by a person that can be used to summon assistance in the event of a medical emergency. A personal safety app with a speech recognition capability, on the other hand, is an application that can identify the user's voice and initiate a response in the event of an emergency or danger.

149. What is the difference between a medical alert system and a personal safety app with motion detection?

A medical alert system is a device that a person wears that can be used to request assistance in the case of a medical emergency, whereas a personal safety app with a motion detection function is an application that can detect motion and prompt a reaction in the event of an emergency or danger.

150. What is the difference between a medical alert system and a biometric-enabled personal safety application?

A medical alert system is a device worn by an individual that can be used to call for help in the event of a medical emergency, whereas a personal safety app with biometric authentication is a mobile app that can authenticate the user's identity using biometric data such as fingerprints or facial recognition.

151. What distinguishes a medical alert system from a personal safety app that includes a panic alarm?

A personal safety app with a panic alarm function is a mobile application that can be used to trigger a loud alarm to draw attention and seek for aid in the event of an emergency or danger.

152. What is the distinction between a medical alert system and a personal safety app with a flashlight?

A medical alert system is a wearable device that may be used to request assistance in the event of a medical emergency, whereas a personal safety app with a flashlight feature is a mobile app that can be used to provide a source of light in the event of an emergency or danger.

153. What is the difference between a medical alert system and a personal safety app that allows you to share your location?

A personal safety app with a location sharing function is a mobile application that may be used to share the user's location with pre-selected contacts or emergency services in the event of an emergency or danger.

154. How does a medical alert system differ from a personal safety app with virtual escort?

A personal safety app with a virtual escort feature is a mobile application that can track the user's location and provide virtual support and guidance in the event of an unsafe situation, whereas a medical alert system is a device worn by an individual that can be used to call for help in the event of a medical emergency.

155. What is the difference between a medical alert system and a personal safety app that includes community safety features?

A personal safety app with a community safety feature is a mobile application that may be used to connect with and receive safety alerts from members of a community or neighborhood.

156. What is the difference between a medical alert system and a personal safety app that includes a chat feature?

In the event of an emergency or danger, a personal safety app with a live chat function is an application that may be installed on a mobile device and used to interact with pre-selected contacts or emergency services in real-time.

157. What is the distinction between a medical alert system and a personal safety app with noise detection?

A medical alert system is a device worn by a person that can be used to summon assistance in the event of a medical emergency. A personal safety app with a noise detection feature, on the other hand, is a mobile device application that can detect loud or unexpected noises and initiate a response in the event of an emergency or danger.

158. What is the difference between a medical alert system and a personal safety app with a weather alert feature?

A personal safety app with a weather alert feature is a mobile application that can be used to receive weather alerts and warnings in the event of severe weather conditions, whereas a medical alert system is a device worn by an individual that can be used to call for help in the event of a medical emergency.

159. What is the difference between a medical alert system and a personal safety app with a power saving feature?

A medical alert system is a device worn by a person that can be used to summon assistance in the event of a medical emergency. A personal safety app with a battery saving feature, on the other hand, is an application that can be loaded on a mobile device and used to maximize the device's battery life in order to ensure that the app is always available in the event of an emergency or danger.

160. What is the difference between a medical alert system and a personal safety app with an emergency contact list?

A personal safety app with an emergency contact list function is a mobile application that may be used to save and rapidly access a list of emergency contacts in the case of an emergency or danger.

161. What is the difference between a medical alert system and a personal safety app with a video recording function?

A medical alert system is a wearable device that may be used to summon assistance in the event of a medical emergency, whereas a personal safety app with video recording capability is a mobile app that can be used to record and save video footage in the event of an emergency or danger.

162. What is the difference between a medical alert system and a personal safety app with a speed dial feature?

A personal safety app with a speed dial feature is an application that can be installed on a mobile device and used to quickly phone pre-selected emergency contacts in the case of an emergency or danger.

163. What is the difference between a medical alert system and a personal safety app with a self-defense feature?

A medical alert system is a device worn by an individual that can be used to summon assistance in the event of a medical emergency, whereas a personal safety app with a self-defense feature is a mobile application that can be used to provide guidance and self-defense tools in the event of an emergency or danger.

164. What is the difference between a medical alert system and a personal safety app with a weather forecast?

A medical alert system is a device worn by a person that can be used to summon assistance in the event of a medical emergency. A personal safety app with a weather forecast function, on the other hand, is an app that can provide weather forecasts and updates to assist users plan their activities safely.

165. What is the difference between a medical alert system and a personal safety app with a road safety feature?

A personal safety app with a road safety feature is an application that can deliver information and warnings about road conditions, traffic, and accidents to help users stay safe when driving or walking.

166. What is the difference between a medical alert system and a personal safety app that includes a translation feature?

A personal safety app with a language translation feature is an application that may translate speech or text in different languages to aid users in communicating successfully in the case of an emergency or danger.

167. What is the difference between a medical alert system and a personal safety app with a first aid advice feature?

A medical alert system is a device worn by a person that can be used to summon assistance in the event of a medical emergency. A personal safety app with a first aid guide function, on the other hand, is a mobile device application that provides information and direction on how to administer first aid in the event of an emergency or injury.

168. What distinguishes a medical alert system from a noise-cancelling personal safety app?

A medical alert system is a device worn by a person that can be used to summon assistance in the event of a medical emergency. A personal safety app with a noise cancellation feature, on the other hand, is an application that can be installed on a mobile device to assist users in hearing and communicating more effectively in the event of an emergency or danger.

169. What is the difference between a medical alert system and a personal safety app with a panic password feature?

A personal safety app with a panic password feature is a mobile device application that may be used to initiate a reaction in the case of an emergency or danger by entering a pre-set panic password.

170. What is the difference between a medical alert system and a personal safety app with an emergency lock screen button?

A personal safety app with an emergency button on the lock screen feature is an application loaded on a mobile device that may be used to initiate a response in the case of an emergency or danger by hitting an emergency button on the lock screen.

171. What's the difference between a medical alert system and a personal safety app with location-based alerts? In the event of an emergency or danger, a personal safety app with a location-based alerts function can be used to send notifications to emergency contacts or authorities based on the user's position.

172. What is the difference between a medical alert system and a personal safety app with a virtual escort feature?

A personal safety app with a virtual escort function is a smartphone application that may be used to provide a virtual escort service to assist users feel safe while walking or traveling alone.

173. What is the difference between a medical alert system and a personal safety app with a community watch function?

A medical alert system is a gadget that a person wears that can be used to call for help in the event of a medical emergency, whereas a personal safety app with a community watch feature is an app that connects users with a community of other users who can help look out for each other's safety.

174. What is the difference between a medical alert system and a personal safety app with a false call feature?

A medical alert system is a device worn by a person that can be used to summon assistance in the event of a medical emergency. A personal safety app with a fake call feature, on the other hand, is an application that can be loaded on a mobile device and used to simulate a phone call to assist users in escaping potentially harmful circumstances.

175. What is the distinction between a medical alert system and a personal safety app with a flashlight?

A medical alert system is a wearable device that may be used to request assistance in the event of a medical emergency, whereas a personal safety app with a flashlight feature is a mobile app that can be used to provide a source of light in the event of an emergency or danger.

176. What's the difference between a medical alert system and a personal safety app with GPS tracking?

A medical alert system is a device worn by a person that can be used to summon assistance in the event of a medical emergency. A personal safety app with GPS tracking, on the other hand, is an app that may track the user's location and send alerts or messages to emergency contacts or authorities in the event of an emergency or danger.

177. How does a medical alert system differ from a personal safety app with an audible alarm?

A personal safety app with a sound alarm function is a mobile application that may be used to trigger a loud sound alarm to attract attention and discourage potential attackers or danger.

178. What is the difference between a medical alert system and a personal safety app with speech recognition?

A medical alert system is a device worn by a person that can be used to summon assistance in the event of a medical emergency. A personal safety app with a speech recognition function, on the other hand, is one that can identify the user's voice and initiate a response or alarm in the event of an emergency or danger.

179. What is the difference between a medical alert system and a personal safety app that includes family locate functionality?

A medical alert system is a device worn by a person that can be used to summon assistance in the event of a medical emergency. A personal safety app with a family locator function is a smartphone application that can track family members' locations and provide alerts or messages in the case of an emergency or danger.

180. What is the difference between a medical alert system and a biometric-enabled personal safety application?

A personal safety app with a biometric authentication feature is a mobile application that may be used to confirm the user's identity using biometric data, such as fingerprints or face recognition, to trigger a response or alarm in the event of an emergency or danger.

181. What is the difference between a medical alert system and a personal safety app that includes two-way communication capabilities?

Answer: A medical alert system is a device worn by an individual that can be used to summon assistance in the event of a medical emergency, whereas a personal safety app with a two-way communication feature is an application installed on a mobile device that can be used to establish a two-way communication channel in the event of an emergency or danger.

182. What is the difference between a medical alert system and a personal safety app with a battery optimization feature?

Answer: A medical alert system is a device that an individual wears that can be used to summon help in the event of a medical emergency, whereas a personal safety app with a battery optimization feature is an application installed on a mobile device that can be used to optimize the device's battery life to ensure that the app is always available in the event of an emergency or danger.

183. What is the difference between a medical alert system and a personal safety app that detects falls?

Answer: A medical alert system is a device worn by an individual that can be used to summon assistance in the event of a medical emergency, whereas a personal safety app with a fall detection feature is a mobile device application that can detect falls and trigger a response or alert in the event of an emergency or danger.

184. How does a medical alert system differ from a personal safety app using facial recognition?

Answer: A medical alert system is a device worn by a person that can be used to summon assistance in the event of a medical emergency, whereas a personal safety app with a facial recognition feature is an application installed on a mobile device that can recognize the user's face and trigger a response or alert in the event of an emergency or danger.

185. What is the difference between a medical alert system and a personal safety software that supports voice commands?

A medical alert system is a device worn by an individual that can be used to summon assistance in the event of a medical emergency, whereas a personal safety app with a voice command feature is an application installed on a mobile device that can be used to trigger a response or alert in the event of an emergency or danger by using voice commands.

186. How does a medical alert system differ from a personal safety app with motion detection?

Answer: A medical alert system is a device worn by an individual that can be used to summon assistance in the event of a medical emergency, whereas a personal safety app with a motion detection feature is a mobile device application that can detect motion and trigger a response or alert in the event of an emergency or danger.

187. How does a medical alert system differ from a personal safety app with remote monitoring?

Answer: A medical alert system is a device worn by an individual that can be used to summon assistance in the event of a medical emergency, whereas a personal safety app with a remote monitoring feature is a mobile device application that can be used to remotely monitor the user's safety and well-being in the event of an emergency or danger.

188. What is the distinction between a medical alert system and a personal safety app that includes a panic button?

Answer: A medical alert system is a device worn by an individual that can be used to call for help in the event of a medical emergency, whereas a personal safety app with a panic button feature is an application installed on a mobile device that can be used to trigger a response or alert in the event of an emergency or danger by tapping a panic button.

189. What is the difference between a medical alert system and a personal safety app with photo sharing features?

Answer: A personal safety app with a photo sharing feature is an application installed on a mobile device that may be used to share photos of potential danger or suspicious activity with emergency contacts or authorities in the case of an emergency or danger.

190. What is the difference between a medical alert system and a personal safety app with live streaming?

Answer: A medical alert system is a device worn by an individual that can be used to summon assistance in the event of a medical emergency, whereas a personal safety app with a live streaming feature is a mobile device application that can be used to stream live video footage to emergency contacts or authorities in the event of an emergency or danger.

191. What is the difference between a medical alert system and a geofenced personal safety app?

Answer: A personal safety app with a geofencing feature is an application installed on a mobile device that may be used to set up virtual boundaries or geofences and trigger a response or alert when the user enters or exits these boundaries in the event of an emergency or danger.

192. What is the difference between a medical alert system and a personal safety app that tracks your location?

A medical alert system is a device worn by an individual that can be used to summon assistance in the event of a medical emergency, whereas a personal safety app with a location tracking feature is an app installed on a mobile device that can track the user's location and trigger a response or alert in the event of an emergency or danger.

193. What is the difference between a medical alert system and a personal safety app with a weather alert?

Answer: A medical alert system is a device worn by an individual that can be used to summon assistance in the event of a medical emergency, whereas a personal safety app with a weather alert feature is a mobile device application that can be used to receive weather alerts and warnings in the event of severe weather conditions that may endanger the user's safety and well-being.

194. What is the difference between a medical alert system and a personal safety app with social media integration?

Answer: A medical alert system is a device worn by an individual that can be used to summon assistance in the event of a medical emergency, whereas a personal safety app with a social media integration feature is a mobile device application that can be used to integrate with social media platforms to share the user's location and safety status with friends or family members in the event of an emergency or danger.

195. How does a medical alert system differ from a personal safety app with speech recognition?

Answer: A medical alert system is a device worn by an individual that can be used to summon assistance in the event of a medical emergency, whereas a personal safety app with a voice recognition feature is an app installed on a mobile device that can recognize the user's voice and trigger a response or alert in the event of an emergency or danger.

196. What is the difference between a medical alert system and a personal safety app that detects noise?

Answer: A medical alert system is a device worn by an individual that can be used to summon assistance in the event of a medical emergency, whereas a personal safety app with a noise detection feature is an application installed on a mobile device that can detect loud or suspicious noises and trigger an emergency or danger response or alert.

197. What's the difference between a medical alert system and a personal safety app with a backup battery?

Answer: A medical alert system is a device worn by an individual that can be used to summon assistance in the event of a medical emergency, whereas a personal safety app with a battery backup feature is a mobile device application that can be used to ensure that the app is always available in the event of an emergency or danger by providing a backup power source.

198. What is the difference between a medical alert system and a personal safety software that supports wearable devices?

A medical alert system is a device worn by an individual that can be used to summon assistance in the event of a medical emergency, whereas a personal safety app with wearable device compatibility is an application that can be installed on a wearable device and can be used to trigger a response or alert in the event of an emergency or danger.

199. What is the difference between a medical alert system and a personal safety app with an emergency contact feature?

Answer: A medical alert system is a device worn by an individual that can be used to summon assistance in the event of a medical emergency, whereas a personal safety app with an emergency contact feature is a mobile device application that can be used to store emergency contact information and trigger a response or alert in the event of an emergency or danger.

200. How does a medical alert system differ from a personal safety app with in-app messaging?

Answer: A medical alert system is a device that an individual wears that can be used to summon assistance in the event of a medical emergency, whereas a personal safety app with an in-app messaging feature is an app installed on a mobile device that can be used to communicate with emergency contacts or authorities in the event of an emergency or danger via an in-app messaging system.

201. What is the difference between a medical alert system and a timed personal safety app?

Answer: A medical alert system is a device worn by an individual that can be used to summon assistance in the event of a medical emergency, whereas a personal safety app with a timer feature is a mobile device application that can be used to set a timer to trigger a response or alert in the event of an emergency or danger.

202. What is the difference between a medical alert system and a personal safety app with an SOS button?

Answer: A medical alert system is a device worn by an individual that can be used to summon assistance in the event of a medical emergency, whereas a personal safety app with an SOS signal feature is a mobile device application that can be used to send an SOS signal to emergency contacts or authorities in the event of an emergency or danger.

203. How does a medical alert system differ from a personal safety app that includes a crowd-sourced safety map?

Answer: A medical alert system is a device worn by an individual that can be used to summon assistance in the event of a medical emergency, whereas a personal safety app with a crowd-sourced safety map feature is a mobile device application that can be used to access a map that displays crowdsourced safety information and incidents in real-time.

204. What is the difference between a medical alert system and a personal safety app with a virtual escort feature?

Answer: A medical alert system is a device worn by an individual that can be used to summon assistance in the event of a medical emergency, whereas a personal safety app with a virtual escort feature is a mobile app that can be used to request a virtual escort to monitor the user's movements and ensure their safety in the event of an emergency or danger.

205. What is the difference between a medical alert system and a personal safety app with a wellness tracking feature?

Answer: A medical alert system is a device worn by an individual that can be used to summon assistance in the event of a medical emergency, whereas a personal safety app with a wellness tracking feature is a mobile app that can be used to track the user's wellness metrics, such as sleep, exercise, and diet, to ensure their overall well-being.

206. What is the difference between a medical alert system and a noise-cancelling personal safety app?

Answer: A medical alert system is a device worn by an individual that can be used to summon assistance in the event of a medical emergency, whereas a personal safety app with a noise-cancelling feature is an app installed on a mobile device that can be used to cancel out background noise to ensure that the user's voice is clearly heard in the event of an emergency or danger.

207. What's the difference between a medical alert system and a personal safety app with a flashlight?

Answer: A personal safety app with a flashlight feature is an application installed on a mobile device that may be utilized to offer a source of light in the case of an emergency or danger in low-light or dark settings.

208. What is the difference between a medical alert system and a personal safety app with self-defense training?

Answer: A medical alert system is a device worn by a person that can be used to summon assistance in the event of a medical emergency, whereas a personal safety app with a self-defense training feature is an application that provides the user with self-defense training and techniques to protect themselves in the event of an emergency or danger.

209. What's the difference between a medical alert system and a personal safety app with GPS tracking?

Answer: A medical alert system is a device worn by a person that can be used to summon help in the event of a medical emergency, whereas a personal safety app with a GPS tracking feature is an application installed on a mobile device that can be used to track the user's location in real-time to ensure their safety in the event of an emergency or danger.

210. What is the difference between a medical alert system and a personal safety app with language translation?

Answer: A personal safety app with a language translation feature is an application loaded on a mobile device that can be used to translate languages in the event of an emergency or danger when communicating with persons who speak a different language.

211. What is the difference between a medical alert system and a personal safety app that allows you to share your location?

Answer: A medical alert system is a device worn by an individual that can be used to summon assistance in the event of a medical emergency, whereas a personal safety app with a location sharing feature is a mobile device application that can be used to share the user's location with designated contacts or authorities in the event of an emergency or danger.

212. What is the difference between a medical alert system and a personal safety app with a panic button?

Answer: A medical alert system is a device worn by an individual that can be used to summon assistance in the event of a medical emergency, whereas a personal safety app with a panic button feature is a mobile device application that can be used to send an immediate alert to emergency contacts or authorities in the event of an emergency or danger.

213. What is the difference between a medical alert system and a personal safety app with a voice-activated feature?

Answer: A medical alert system is a device worn by an individual that can be used to summon assistance in the event of a medical emergency, whereas a personal safety app with a voice-activated feature is a mobile device application that can be activated by the user's voice to trigger an alert or response in the event of an emergency or danger.

214. What is the difference between a medical alert system and a personal safety app with a virtual assistant?

Answer: A medical alert system is a device that a person wears that can be used to call for help in the event of a medical emergency, whereas a personal safety app with a virtual assistant feature is an application installed on a mobile device that can provide assistance and guidance in emergency situations or help the user stay safe during daily activities.

215. What is the difference between a medical alert system and a personal safety app with real-time video streaming?

Answer: A medical alert system is a device worn by an individual that can be used to summon assistance in the event of a medical emergency, whereas a personal safety app with a real-time video streaming feature is a mobile app that can stream live video to designated contacts or authorities in the event of an emergency or danger.

216. How does a medical alert system differ from a personal safety app with automated fall detection?

A medical alert system is a device worn by an individual that can be used to summon assistance in the event of a medical emergency, whereas a personal safety app with an automatic fall detection feature is a mobile device application that can detect falls and send an alert to emergency contacts or authorities in the event of a fall-related emergency.

217. What is the difference between a medical alert system and a personal safety app with heart rate monitoring?

Answer: A medical alert system is a device worn by a person that can be used to summon help in the event of a medical emergency, whereas a personal safety app with a heart rate monitoring feature is an application installed on a mobile device that can monitor the user's heart rate in real-time to detect and respond to potential medical emergencies.

218. What is the difference between a medical alert system and a personal safety app with a weather alert feature?

Answer: A medical alert system is a device that a person wears that can be used to summon help in the event of a medical emergency, whereas a personal safety app with a weather alert feature is an application installed on a mobile device that can provide real-time weather alerts to help the user stay safe in hazardous weather conditions.

219. What's the difference between a medical alert system and a personal safety app with a wireless panic button?

A medical alert system is a device worn by an individual that can be used to summon help in the event of a medical emergency, whereas a personal safety app with a wireless panic button feature is an app installed on a mobile device that can send an alert to emergency contacts or authorities via a wireless button or remote control.

220. What is the difference between a medical alert system and a personal safety app that includes speech recognition?

A medical alert system is a device worn by an individual that can be used to summon help in the event of a medical emergency, whereas a personal safety app with a voice recognition feature is an app installed on a mobile device that can recognize the user's voice to trigger an alert or response in the event of an emergency or danger.

221. What is the difference between a medical alert system and a personal safety app with an automatic messaging feature?

Answer: A medical alert system is a device worn by an individual that can be used to summon assistance in the event of a medical emergency, whereas a personal safety app with an automatic message feature is a mobile device application that can send an automatic message to designated contacts or authorities in the event of an emergency or danger.

222. What is the difference between a medical alert system and a personal safety app with GPS location history?

Answer: A medical alert system is a device worn by an individual that can be used to summon help in the event of a medical emergency, whereas a personal safety app with a GPS location history feature is a mobile app that can track the user's location history to provide insights and information about their movements and safety.

223. What is the difference between a medical alert system and a personal safety app with a speed dial function?

Answer: A medical alert system is a device worn by an individual that can be used to summon assistance in the event of a medical emergency, whereas a personal safety app with a speed dial feature is a mobile device application that can provide quick access to emergency contacts or authorities in the event of an emergency or danger.

224. What is the difference between a medical alert system and a personal safety app that includes remote monitoring?

Answer: A medical alert system is a device worn by a person that can be used to summon help in the event of a medical emergency, whereas a personal safety app with a remote monitoring feature is an application that can be used to remotely monitor the user's safety, using sensors or cameras, and trigger an alert or response in the event of an emergency or danger.

225. What distinguishes a medical alert system from a personal safety app with a reminder function?

Answer: A medical alert system is a device that a person wears that can be used to summon help in the event of a medical emergency, whereas a personal safety app with a reminder feature is an application installed on a mobile device that can provide reminders to the user to help them stay safe and avoid potential dangers.

226. What is the difference between a medical alert system and a personal safety app with a family locator?

Answer: A medical alert system is a gadget worn by an individual that may be used to summon help in the event of a medical emergency, whereas a personal safety app with a family locator feature is a mobile app that can track the position of family members to ensure their safety and well-being.

227. What is the difference between a medical alert system and a personal safety app with a medical history feature?

Answer: A medical alert system is a device worn by an individual that can be used to summon help in the event of a medical emergency, whereas a personal safety app with a medical history feature is a mobile app that can access the user's medical history to ensure they receive the appropriate medical care in the event of an emergency.

228. What is the difference between a medical alert system and a personal safety app that includes habit tracking?

Answer: A medical alert system is a device worn by an individual that can be used to summon assistance in the event of a medical emergency, whereas a personal safety app with a habit tracking feature is a mobile device application that can track the user's habits and behaviors to ensure their overall well-being and safety.

229. What is the difference between a medical alert system and a personal safety app with a driving mode feature?

A personal safety app with a driving mode feature is an application loaded on a mobile device that can help the user stay safe while driving by reducing distractions and delivering alerts in the event of an emergency or danger.

230. What is the difference between a medical alert system and a personal safety app with a panic alarm?

Answer: A medical alert system is a device worn by an individual that can be used to summon assistance in the event of a medical emergency, whereas a personal safety app with a panic alarm feature is a mobile device application that can sound a loud alarm to attract attention and deter potential attackers or danger.

231. What is the difference between a medical alert system and a personal safety app that includes crisis management features?

Answer: A medical alert system is a device worn by an individual that can be used to summon help in the event of a medical emergency, whereas a personal safety app with a crisis management feature is an application that provides the user with guidance and support in the event of a crisis or emergency situation.

232. What is the difference between a medical alert system and a personal safety app with a push notification feature?

A medical alert system is a device that a person wears that can be used to summon help in the event of a medical emergency, whereas a personal safety app with a push notification feature is an application that sends real-time notifications to the user's mobile device, alerting them to potential dangers or emergencies in their area.

233. What is the difference between a medical alert system and a personal safety app with a check-in feature?

Answer: A medical alert system is a device that a person wears that can be used to summon help in the event of a medical emergency, whereas a personal safety app with a check-in feature is an application that allows the user to check in and provide updates on their safety and location to designated contacts or authorities.

234. What is the difference between a medical alert system and a personal safety app with virtual escort?

Answer: A medical alert system is a device that a person wears that can be used to summon help in the event of a medical emergency, whereas a personal safety app with a virtual escort feature is an application that provides the user with virtual companionship and support while traveling in potentially dangerous areas.

235. What is the difference between a medical alert system and a personal safety app with a community safety feature?

Answer: A medical alert system is a device worn by a person that can be used to summon help in the event of a medical emergency, whereas a personal safety app with a community safety feature is an application that allows users to connect with a community of other users to share safety tips and information and report potential dangers in their area.

236. What is the difference between a medical alert system and a personal safety app that detects noise?

Answer: A medical alert system is a device worn by an individual that can be used to summon assistance in the event of a medical emergency, whereas a personal safety app with a noise detection feature is an application that detects loud or sudden noises that may indicate danger or an emergency using the microphone on the user's mobile device.

237. What's the difference between a medical alert system and a personal safety app with a flashlight?

Answer: A medical alert system is a device that is worn by an individual and can be used to summon assistance in the event of a medical emergency, whereas a personal safety app with a flashlight feature is an application that provides a flashlight function on the user's mobile device to help them navigate in the dark or signal for help.

238. What is the difference between a medical alert system and a personal safety app with a weather alert feature?

Answer: A medical alert system is a device that a person wears that can be used to summon help in the event of a medical emergency, whereas a personal safety app with a weather alert feature is an application that provides real-time updates on weather conditions in the user's area to help them stay safe and prepared for potential weather-related emergencies.

239. What is the difference between a medical alert system and a personal safety app with trip planning capabilities?

Answer: A medical alert system is a device that a person wears that can be used to summon help in the event of a medical emergency, whereas a personal safety app with a journey planning feature is an application that assists users in planning safe routes and transportation options for their travel in order to avoid potentially dangerous areas.

240. What is the distinction between a medical alert system and a personal safety app that includes a false call feature?

Answer: A medical alert system is a gadget that a person wears and can be used to call for help in the event of a medical emergency, whereas a personal safety app with a fake call feature is an app that allows the user to simulate a phone call to dissuade potential attackers or danger.

241. What differentiates a CPC from a CCS? 242.

A professional who holds an AAPC certification and specializes in outpatient coding is known as a CPC, whereas an individual holding an AHIMA certification and focusing on inpatient coding is known as a CCS.

What function does a medical coder play in the healthcare sector?

The assignment of medical codes to patient diagnoses and treatments for billing purposes is the responsibility of a medical coder.

244. What does medical coding serve?

To accurately record and communicate patient diagnoses and treatments for billing and reimbursement purposes is the goal of medical coding.

245. What is a codebook, exactly?

A codebook is a reference book that lists medical codes along with the descriptions that go with them.

246. What is the CPT codebook, number 246?

In order to report medical operations and services, medical codes are contained in the CPT codebook, a reference guide.

247. What is the ICD codebook, number 247?

In order to report patient diagnoses and other medical problems, medical codes are found in the ICD codebook, a reference guide.

248. What is the HCPCS codebook, number 248? The HCPCS codebook is a reference guide that includes medical codes for disclosing treatments and services that are not CPT-covered.

249. What does a modifier do?

In order to provide more details on a medical process or service, a modifier is a two-digit code.

250. What does an E/M code mean?

An E/M code is a medical designation for services in evaluation and management.

251. What exactly is a bundled code?

A bundled code is a medical term for several procedures or services that are frequently rendered together and are not reported individually.

252 What does unbundling entail?

The act of reporting multiple medical codes for operations or services that should only be recorded under a single bundled code is known as unbundling.

253. What is a charge schedule?

A fee schedule is a list of the costs associated with various medical treatments and services.

254. What does reimbursement rate mean?

The amount that a healthcare professional is paid for a procedure or service is known as a reimbursement rate.

255. What is a denial code?

A denial code is a code that an insurance provider uses to show that a medical claim has been rejected.

256. What is an appeal of a claim?

The procedure by which a healthcare practitioner can contest an insurance claim denial is called a claim appeal.

257. What is a medical biller's function?

A medical biller's duties include submitting medical claims to insurance providers and handling payments from both parties, including patients and insurers.

258. What is a clearinghouse, exactly?

An institution that handles and communicates medical claims between insurance companies and healthcare providers is known as a clearinghouse.

259. What is a compliance plan, exactly?

A compliance strategy is a set of guidelines intended to make sure that healthcare practitioners follow moral and legal requirements when they bill and code.

260. What constitutes fraud?

The deliberate misrepresenting of information for financial benefit constitutes fraud.

261. What is abuse, exactly?

The improper or excessive use of resources or services is referred to as abuse.

262. What exactly is the False Claims Act?

The False Claims Act is a federal statute that punishes individuals or organizations who make false or fraudulent claims to the government for reimbursement.

263. What exactly is the Stark Law?

The Stark Statute is a federal regulation that prohibits healthcare practitioners from referring patients to organizations with which they have financial ties in order for them to acquire certain defined health services.

264. Article, what is the Anti-Kickback Statute?

The Anti-Kickback Statute prohibits healthcare providers from providing or accepting payment in exchange for recommendations for medical services or goods.

265. What exactly is the Health Insurance Portability and Accountability Act (HIPAA)?

The federal statute known as HIPAA sets privacy and security requirements for protected health information.

266. What is a compliance audit, exactly?

A compliance audit examines a healthcare provider's billing and coding procedures to make sure they adhere to the law and moral principles.

267. What is a compliance officer's job description?

The purpose of a compliance officer is to guarantee that a healthcare provider's billing and coding procedures adhere to all applicable laws and moral guidelines.

268. What is a coding audit, exactly?

An examination of a healthcare provider's medical coding procedures to guarantee accuracy and adherence to coding standards is known as a coding audit.

269 What does a coding auditor do?

A coding auditor's job is to examine a healthcare provider's medical coding procedures to guarantee correctness and adherence to coding standards.

270. What distinguishes an audit from a review?

A review is a less thorough investigation that concentrates on particular areas of concern, whereas an audit is a thorough investigation of a healthcare provider's billing and coding methods.

271. What does a compliance plan assessment entail?

A compliance plan assessment looks at a healthcare provider's compliance plan to make sure it's current and effective.

272. What is a compliance plan assessor's job description?

A compliance plan assessor's job is to look over a healthcare provider's compliance plan and make sure it's current and functional.

273. What is the OIG, exactly?

A government organization called the OIG (Office of Inspector General) is in charge of guarding against waste, fraud, and abuse in federal healthcare programs.

274. What part does the OIG play in healthcare coding and billing?

The OIG's responsibility is to look into and bring legal action against instances of healthcare billing and coding fraud, waste, and abuse.

275. What is the Medicare Fraud Strike Force, paragraph?

The OIG and the Department of Justice collaborate on the Medicare Fraud Strike Force, which looks into and prosecutes incidents of healthcare fraud.

276. What is the difference between fraud and abuse in healthcare coding and billing?

The difference between fraud and abuse is how resources or services are used improperly or excessively. Fraud is defined as the intentional misrepresenting of information for personal gain.

277. What is a compliance hotline, exactly?

A compliance hotline is a phone number that staff members can utilize to report potential legal or ethical transgressions.

278. What does a compliance training program entail?

A compliance training program educates healthcare professionals on the moral and legal requirements for billing and coding.

279. What is a compliance trainer's job description?

The purpose of a compliance trainer is to inform medical professionals about the moral and legal requirements for coding and billing.

280. What is a coding manual, number 280?

A coding manual is a guidebook that offers recommendations and instructions for allocating medical codes.

281. Describe the CCI.

The CCI (Correct Coding Initiative) is a program that uses bundling codes that are normally executed simultaneously and not independently reportable to identify and prevent inappropriate coding practices.

282 Describe the NCCI.

In order to stop erroneous coding practices, Medicare and other government payers use the NCCI (National Correct Coding Initiative), a variation of the CCI.

283. What is a coding compliance program, exactly? 283.

A coding compliance program is a collection of guidelines created to guarantee that medical coding processes adhere to moral and legal requirements.

284. A coding compliance officer is what? 284.

A coding compliance officer's responsibility is to make sure that medical coding procedures adhere to moral and legal obligations.

285. What is a program for coding audits?

A coding audit program examines medical coding procedures to guarantee accuracy and adherence to coding standards.

286. What is a coding audit plan, exactly?

A coding audit plan is a document that defines the steps and requirements for carrying out a code audit program.

287. What is a coding audit team, exactly?

A team of people charged with carrying out a coding audit program is known as a coding audit team.

288. What function does a coding audit team perform?

A coding audit team's job is to examine medical coding procedures to ensure their accuracy and adherence to coding standards.

289. What is a plan for coding compliance?

A strategy that specifies the policies and procedures for ensuring that medical coding methods adhere to moral and ethical guidelines is known as a coding compliance plan.

290. What is an evaluation of a coding compliance program?

An evaluation of the efficacy and relevance of a healthcare provider's coding compliance program is known as a coding compliance program assessment.

291. What does an assessor for a coding compliance program do?

A coding compliance program assessor's job is to look through a healthcare provider's coding compliance program and make sure it's current and effective.

292. What distinguishes a coding compliance program from a coding audit program?

While a coding compliance program is a collection of policies and processes intended to ensure that medical coding activities adhere to moral and ethical standards, a coding audit program examines medical coding practices to assess accuracy and conformity with coding guidelines.

293. What does a manager of code compliance do?

Assuring that a healthcare provider's coding compliance program meets with moral and legal requirements is the responsibility of a code compliance manager.

294. What typical coding mistakes may a coding compliance application assist prevent? 294.

Unbundling, upcoding, and downcoding are typical coding errors that a coding compliance tool can assist prevent.

295. What is upcoding?

The act of assigning a higher-level medical code than what the supporting documentation in the medical record allows is known as upcoding.

296. What is downcoding, exactly?

The act of assigning a lower-level medical code than what the supporting documentation in the medical record allows is known as downcoding.

297. A checklist for coding compliance is what?

A healthcare practitioner can utilize a checklist called a "coding compliance checklist" to make sure that their coding procedures adhere to moral and legal requirements.

298. What does a risk assessment for coding compliance entail?

A coding compliance risk assessment examines a healthcare provider's coding procedures to spot any potential infractions of the law and moral obligations.

299. A code compliance audit report is what, exactly?

A coding compliance audit report is a written summary of the results of a coding audit program that includes suggestions for bettering coding procedures.

300. What is an action plan for coding compliance?

A plan that describes the activities a healthcare provider will take to remedy any areas of noncompliance noted in a coding compliance audit report is known as an action plan for coding compliance.

Two bonus video courses to improve your chances with the CPC Exam

Made in the USA
Las Vegas, NV
17 September 2023

77731473R00059